IN SEARCH OF BIRDS IN MID WALES

BRIAN O'SHEA
AND
JOHN GREEN

ILLUSTRATIONS BY JOHN GREEN

We would like to acknowledge the help given by various friends in reading checking and correcting the manuscript but in particular we wish to thank Peter Davies, ornithologist for the Nature Conservancy Council of Wales, and Bird Recorder for Ceredigion for very kindly reading the draft and making invaluable suggestions and corrections. We alone, though, remain responsible for any errors which may have slipped through.

Illustrations by John Green
Front: Red Kite. Back: Stonechat.
Book design Michal Bończa
Published by Artery Publications 1988
11 Dorset Road, London W5 4HU
Typesetting by Lasso, London N7
ISBN 0 9513909 0 2
Printed by The Cambrian News, Aberystwyth

IN SEARCH OF BIRDS IN MID WALES

BRIAN O'SHEA
AND
JOHN GREEN

ILLUSTRATIONS BY JOHN GREEN

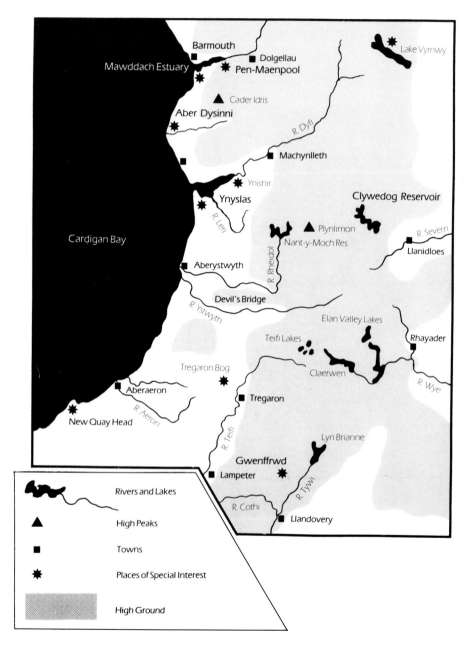

Barmouth

Mawddach Estuary

Dolgellau

Pen-Maenpool

Cader Idris

Aber Dysinni

Machynlleth

Ynishir

Ynyslas

R. Dyfi

Clywedog Reservoir

R. Leri

Cardigan Bay

Plynlimon

Nant-y-Moch Res.

R. Severn

Llanidloes

R. Rheidol

Aberystwyth

Devil's Bridge

R. Ystwyth

Elan Valley Lakes

Teifi Lakes

Rhayader

Tregaron Bog

Claerwen

R. Wye

Aberaeron

Tregaron

R. Aeron

New Quay Head

R. Teifi

Lyn Brianne

Gwenffrwd

Lampeter

R. Tywi

R. Cothi

Llandovery

Lake Vyrnwy

Rivers and Lakes

High Peaks

Towns

Places of Special Interest

High Ground

INTRODUCTION

In today's world real excitement and the thrill of adventure is not easy to find.

Our cities and industries are increasingly encroaching on what remains of our countryside; commercialised farming has seen thousands of miles of hedgerows disappear along with woodlands, marshes and common land. Fences and 'private property' notices are going up continually. The greed for profit at any cost has led to the dangerous overuse of pesticides, chemical fertilisers, and the mechanisation of much farming practice, all of which have had disastrous effects on our plant and animal life. We have seen species disappear and others reduced to dangerously low numbers, and the vigilance of organisations such as the Royal Society for the Protection of Birds and the Royal Society for Nature Conservation is constantly needed to help protect our wild life together with the goodwill of farmers, landowners and forestry authorities and many others with power to influence the environment in which plant and animal life must flourish.

Although there is no room for complacency with sprawling spruce forests, the loss of heather, the drainage of wetlands and the chopping down of fine woodlands, mid Wales, because of its low population and its wealth of relatively undisturbed natural havens for wildlife, is a rare naturalist's paradise.

Here you can escape the confines of brick and concrete prisons and roam free over the unfenced valleys and hills. You can become a wild life detective, trying to track down, identify and observe the bird life hidden or inconspicuous to the casual visitor. Here you can recapture that lost sense of excitement and adventure as you pit your wits against the secretive and wily birds of the area.

Our aim in writing this booklet is to interest both those who know little about birds as well as those with an established ornithological interest, in the hope of helping both to get more enjoyment from mid Wales and its bird life. We also hope that this book will encourage the reader to respect and love wild birds and the environment in which they live, and will actively support efforts to protect our countryside.

After many enjoyable bird watching holidays in the area I made my home in the Ystwyth valley in 1984. My friend, co-author and illustrator John Green, lives in London but frequently joins me on bird watching expeditions and has, with me, attempted to pass on to the reader information, hints and tips about the birds to be seen here.

The emphasis of the book is very much on those birds breeding in the area, which can be seen during the spring and summer months. Only limited reference is made to winter birdwatching and passage migrants.

Our efforts have been concentrated on North Ceredigion and the adjoining districts of Montgomery, Radnor, Brecon and Carmarthen. Our mid Wales map on page 4 however covers a larger area (not including eastern areas of Powys), and to an extent our comments on frequency and distribution intend to cover the whole area. In a given habitat the birds encountered are generally similar from one part of mid Wales to another although eastern areas have more 'lowland birds' and miss out on other species or hold them in fewer numbers.

Whilst it is true that a full day's bird watching in west Wales in May might produce 100 species, over large areas some of the interesting birds have to be sought with purpose and a sense of where to look for them. There are few places where you can watch large numbers of birds on passage as you can in Norfolk, or wander along country lanes throbbing with the song of small birds as you can, say, in parts of Hampshire or Warwickshire. Here in Wales densities of birds tend to be lower, particularly on higher ground. Searching for rare and exciting species in the setting of superb

scenery however, can give great pleasure and has inspired the title of this book.

Of course whilst some species do require some determination to find others can be readily observed from the car parked on a mountain road or picnic area by the river. For those less mobile it is quite easy to observe dippers, grey wagtails or small song birds at numerous riverside stopping places. Buzzard and kites can be watched regularly from the road as they circle the wooded hills or farmlands. Only last month I saw kite, buzzard, kestrel and sparrow hawk within a space of three minutes from a hill road dotted here and there with mountain ash.

The real strength of mid Wales lies in the variety of its breeding species. Around 125 different birds nest annually and another 10 or so do sparingly or have done in the past 15 years.

In this book we have concentrated on those species which are most typical for the area, more numerous here than in other locations and interesting rarities which people come to see from far afield. Foremost amongst these is of course the red kite, but other birds of prey are just as exciting as are species like the chough, pied flycatcher or raven.

There are very few publications covering bird life in mid Wales in contrast to, for instance, the wealth of literature on the birds of the Scottish Highlands.

There are the *Birds of Cardiganshire* by Ingram, Morrey-Salmon and Condry, and other county guides by the same authors. There is the *Guide to the Birds of Wales* by David Saunders which treats each county individually, and a comprehensive recent publication produced by the Dyfed Wildlife Trust, *The Nature of West Wales* which deals with the whole range of plant and animal life and the environment which supports them in the county of Dyfed. There are smaller booklets such as Martin Peers' *Birds of Radnorshire and Mid Powys* and some annual bird reports although these are often published only intermittently. We have drawn freely on such reports and publications to supplement our own observations and information.

The birds are dealt with by habitat. In this way the visitor can refer to the text and see what he might expect to see with a little luck and effort. In practice of course he or she will normally have the benefit of a combination of habitats in almost any vicinity which obviously increases the range of birds which may be seen.

In the sections of this book we have tried to create an atmosphere of the place and experience of the birds as you find them in their natural haunts. Our descriptions of the species are not meant as a means of identification since you will need a good guide for that. Throughout the book we try to relate that sense of adventure and excitement involved in bird watching and the 'in search of' sections are particularly designed for this purpose.

The references to status, range and distribution will, we hope, not only be of interest, but also help you to find the birds more easily. At the end of the book you will find a systematic list of all birds breeding in mid Wales. We have attempted to assess their degree of rarity on a 5 point scale and indicate in which habitat they are normally found.

THE AREA

Mid Wales is without doubt one of the most beautiful parts of Britain. The whole region is hilly, with winding narrow roads, and divided by thickly wooded valleys which echo to the chortling and cascading of fast flowing rivers and crystal clear streams.

It is true there are few high peaks except in the north where the well known Cader Idris and other peaks such as Aran Fawddwy reach nearly 900 metres.

The high ground at around 500 metres is moorland grass interspersed with clumps of rush and patches of sodden, spongy sphagnum moss. Here and there are small pools and numerous gullies gushing with small streams.

On wet days with the dark clouds invading the hill tops in its desolate emptiness the effect can be forbidding, but in fine weather the clean, crisp air can be bracing and the wide open spaces convey an exhilarating sense of freedom.

On the poorer soils of the higher altitudes there are a few isolated grey farmsteads but most of these are already derelict monuments to a failed struggle for a livelihood against the winds and rains.

Leaving the moors we descend into wooded valleys of hanging sessile oakwoods via rocky gorges and ravines. The oaks cling stubbornly to the rocky, steep-sided valleys, their trunks often swathed in velvety-green moss, allowing small ferns to gain a foothold, giving an almost tropical aura.

The woods are carpeted with moss and bracken, often with little undergrowth save for some grass and a little scraggy bramble. These then give way in the lower valleys to more varied woodlands dominated by the common oak and beech.

On the farmland at lower altitudes the soil is richer and the vegetation greener, especially east of the Cambrian Mountains, with many idyllic scenes of a fairy tale beauty, as pretty as any in the more fashionable parts of South West England. Recently I drove direct from South Devon to mid Wales and for my money the latter compared and contrasted very favourably with that more trodden, travelled and celebrated region to the south of the Bristol Channel.

Dairy, beef cattle, and of course, sheep farming are the dominant forms of agricultural activity and the many country lanes of this lower, but still hilly landscape, provide enjoyable, relatively traffic-free walks. In the spring the hedgerows become a flowering garden of celandines, primroses, violets and later bluebells, fox-gloves and honeysuckle.

In the west the farmland belt is narrower in the north where mountains close in on the sea but broader in the south. Here the fields are often invaded with rush and reed but they are generally not rich in bird life. The largest of these marshes or bogs is some five miles long just north of Tregaron.

Both to the east and west of the main chain of hills and spreading over them are the plantations of spruce and larch, threatening the very existence of the moorlands and indirectly increasing the acidity of its lakes and rivers, damaging to the life within them. There has been little attempt to break the monotony by interspersing deciduous trees and the closely planted rows, as they grow, soon cut off the light to the undergrowth, creating impenetrable miles of darkness and silence.

Despite this spread of evergreens there are still many majestic woods of oak and beech in the area, offering cover and food to our summer visitors.

Ceredigion, now a county district of Dyfed, and formerly the county of Cardiganshire, is bounded by a magnificent coastline extending for 50 miles. From high vantage points near Aberystwyth you can look out over the concave sweep of Cardigan Bay from the Lleyn Peninsula in the north to Pembrokeshire in the south. The coast is mostly unspoiled with miles of rugged cliffs scooped and gouged as if by a giant spoon. There are some beautiful beaches in the south, some shingle shoreline from Aberaeron north while at Ynyslas there are dunes extending into the county of Gwynedd near Tywyn, just across the Dyfi estuary.

Only occasionally is the scene interrupted by small towns; New Quay a fishing centre turned popular holiday resort, Aberaeron with its quaint harbour and Aberystwyth, the largest coastal town in the area with a population of 10,000, only inflated temporarily by the student intake at the University and summer holiday makers, making it a lively hub.

The town is almost jostled into the sea by the surrounding hills. Its narrow streets around the old castle ruins are thronged at weekends as shoppers from the countryside carry out their weekly purchases. It nestles cosily at the confluence of the rivers Ystwyth and Rheidol whose valleys wind back up into the surrounding hills.

A few miles to the north lie the flat lands near Borth with the marshes of Cors Fochno to the south of the Dyfi estuary which claims so many of the visiting rarities.

The total population of Ceredigion is only about 62,000 and those of the other county districts of mid Wales are equally sparse. The county of Powys (consisting of Montgomery, Radnor and Brecon) with a total population of only 105,000 is, not without some justification, known as the green desert.

stonechat

Town populations can be numbered in mere thousands with only the thriving centre of Newtown approximating 10,000 inhabitants. The whole area is unsullied by the eyesores of modern industrial or suburban sprawl and can offer a tranquility and peacefulness not easily found in most areas of Britain today.

The Cambrian Mountains which dominate the area provide a wilderness as remote as any outside the Scottish Highlands and in comparison are much more accessible to most of our city regions.

Motoring along the A44 from Leominster, over the Welsh border and westwards, traffic jams are rarer than the peregrine falcon even at the height of the tourist season. This, unlike North Wales, is perhaps partly due to the absence of many sandy beaches.

With so much land in Britain today being fenced off, footpaths being ploughed up and countryside falling into the hands of developers, it is wonderful to be able to wander the hills and valleys of central Wales in almost complete freedom.

'Trespassers will be prosecuted' or 'private property' notices are seldom seen and the Welsh farmers themselves are not unusually restrictive about people walking on their land, providing normal courtesies are maintained, fences and crops are respected, and gates closed behind you. Where in doubt though do ask since farmers have their livelihood to earn and inconsiderate behaviour does nothing to improve the image of either tourists or birdwatchers. As a rule it is best to stick to recognised paths and tracks on any land which is subject to significant farming or forestry use.

Game keeping is little practised in Wales so that apart from giving nature lovers more access it also encourages the birds of prey which are here more numerous than anywhere else in Britain. Seven or eight species breed, a figure only perhaps exceeded in some parts of Scotland.

Birds are by no means the only wild life of interest in the region. The fierce polecat, once nearly extinct and confined to the Aberystwyth district, is now increasing steadily and the perky red squirrel and rare pine marten are struggling to survive and both can be seen occasionally. Otters are still to be met with on mid Wales waters.

In the following pages birds are described as they are found in their habitats which are divided into seven natural types. These obviously interflow or overlap but as we have indicated one or other habitat tends to predominate in a given geographical area.

The **COASTLINE** is clear cut and includes the narrow shore, cliffs and immediate hinterland.

MARSH AND ESTUARY. The main estuary is the Dyfi, but there is also the Mawddach Estuary west of Dolgellau in the extreme north of our area. This incidentally with its wooded slopes and dramatic hills is reckoned by many to be amongst the most beautiful places in Wales. Cors Fochno on the south side of the Dyfi, and Tregaron Bog are two of the largest marsh areas which are found in the river systems, more commonly in the west. The lowland lakes, few as they are, are often associated with marshland and we include them in this section.

FARMS AND FIELDS. This habitat is somewhat harder to define but corresponds to the land bounded by hedgerows, fences and trees, along with unbordered grassed hillsides which may be above 400 metres. Small woods, copses, lanes and villages are scattered over this farmland and we encompass them under this heading. Except in some river valleys and near the coast, few fields are flat enough to, say, contain a football pitch and fields of crops are rare.

UPLAND LAKES AND RIVERS. This includes the largest upland lakes and reservoirs down to the smaller peatpools. The rivers are generally fairly shallow and fast flowing, entering the sea in the West after relatively short journeys from the hills. In the east they enter the major rivers like the Severn and Wye or southwards into the Tywi or Teifi.

VALLEY AND UPLAND WOODS. This takes in the oak woods of the river valleys, other deciduous woods and mixed woods including some evergreen.

CONIFER PLANTATIONS. These are the commercial plantations of spruce, larch and pine, either privately owned or under the Forestry Commission. The trees may vary in height from less than a metre high up to 10 metres or more; and the bird life in them varies accordingly.

Redstart
Whinchat
Wheatear

THE HIGH GROUND includes those areas characterised by moor, rough grassland and rocky crags generally over 350 metres. The majority of this land lies along the central Cambrian spine (shaded on the map).

THE COASTLINE

As already mentioned much of the mid Wales coastline south of **Borth** is made up of high cliffs with a very narrow, pebbly shore.

On a fine day a cliff top walk can be a memorable experience and it is still surprising how few people you meet, considering how invigorating and full of interest such walks can be.

If you rest for a while on a grassy hummock during a cliff top walk and simply contemplate your surroundings you will be surprised what life there is in broom or gorse thickets around you. You will hear the twittering of linnets which love the gorse to nest in, or watch a stonechat perch daintily atop the bushes.

On the rocks below you will see cormorants, herring gulls, oystercatchers and the little rock pipit flitting between the rock pools in search of flies. Where the cliffs are steeper you will see the wheeling fulmars and maybe the chough, though most of the 'black crows' you see will prove to be carrion crows, jackdaws or ravens.

Both to the north and south of **Aberystwyth** are splendid cliffs to wander by and the narrow footpaths are easy to follow. There are sizable herring gull colonies along with the odd pair of great black backs. The cormorant and fulmar breed at mixed sea bird colonies at places like **Wallog**, and **Monks Cave**.

At nearby **Penderi** which is owned by the West Wales Trust for Nature Conservation, there is a large colony of seabirds, including about 15 or 20 pairs of shags and several times this number of cormorants.

There is also a cormorant colony six miles inland at **Craig yr Aderyn** near **Tywyn** which is the only inland colony of this species in England and Wales. Incidentally there was, and it may still be there, a chough's nesting site in a cliff high above the colony of cormorants.

Apart from the colourful and vociferous piping oystercatcher, waders are scarce along the Ceredigion coast where the shore is narrow and unsuitable but at **Ynyslas** there is still a colony of about

fulmar

half a dozen pairs of ringed plovers breeding on the shingle and sand. The dunes are protected as a reserve under the Nature Conservancy Council and here and in the **Borth** area generally a greater variety of birds may be seen near the shore, including sanderling, dunlin and godwits on migration. Gannets, manx shearwaters and red-throated divers and scoters are commonly seen out at sea, the latter two during winter months. Northwards of Towyn is Aberdysynni, which is also an excellent point from which to observe migrating birds or winter visitors. Eider ducks are often here throughout much of the year but in autumn and winter up to 50 can be seen regularly. A hundred or more cormorants and nearly as many shelduck sit along the mudflats of Broadwater in late summer.

This stretch of coast between Aberdyfi and the Mawddach estuary is low lying with a sprinkling of dunes and shingle banks, very much to the liking of oyster catchers and ringed plovers. The little tern also has a toe hold but all three species are under strong pressure from holiday makers who all too often wander clumsily into their nesting territories without even being aware of the birds' presence or the damage they may accidently cause: the birds may desert or leave their eggs for too long, making them infertile, young chicks may remain unfed and unattended eggs or chicks are ready prey for the ever watchful crows and gulls which pose the greatest danger.

At **Aberystwyth** small numbers of purple sandpipers can be seen foraging in the seaweed covered rocks in winter and turnstones are also a regular sight.

Incidentally the black redstart is also seen frequently in the winter months at Aberystwyth, Tywyn and other places along the coast.

The coast of **New Quay** is better for seabirds, and **New Quay Head**, a mile south of the town, has breeding colonies of razorbills and guillemots. There are about 100 pairs of razorbills and probably ten times that number of guillemots on more exposed ledges at **Bird Rock** which is the best place for seabirds on the Ceredigion coast. Both species breed at other sites between here and the **Teifi** estuary at **Cardigan**. The kittiwake, one of our prettiest gulls with its coal black wing tips and ivory white head, is also found at **New Quay Head** and one or two other places notably **Ynys Lochtyn** where there are up to about a hundred pairs. Shags and cormorants are to be found on several cliffs and there are rock doves breeding on the cliffs though, as elsewhere in most of Britain, these are of feral mixed stock. Since it first bred in 1947 the fulmar is now well distributed with over 250 occupied sites. It is easily recognised from the gulls as it sails effortlessly on stiff wings in the thermals near the cliffs.

Any good day's walk along the cliffs should produce a sighting of peregrines in the breeding season. There are at least a dozen pairs along the Ceredigion coastline. This bird was almost extinct along this coast only 20 years ago but it is now thankfully on the increase again, probably because the more harmful agricultural pesticides have been withdrawn from use.

Like the peregrine the chough is also scattered along the coast with a similar number of breeding pairs. The Welsh coast is now the only mainland haunt of this species in Great Britain though there are more in Ireland. A few pairs also breed at inland sites and I have twice seen parties of four in late Summer within two or three miles of **Devils Bridge**.

In search of Chough and Peregrine

Before coming to live in mid Wales it took me some time to see a chough, although they are not shy birds and their habitat choice is circumscribed. Of course, if you aren't looking for them specifically it would be easy to pass them off as crows or jackdaws at a distance. The important thing perhaps, is knowing where to look for them. They like good steep cliffs, usually with a backcloth of steep bracken slopes. A few pairs are usually found in the neighbourhood of Aberystwyth and one site is a particularly romantic and rugged cliff-face.

After leaving our car in a layby we make towards the sea through two fields and out onto the rough ground leading to the cliffs.

This area consists of bracken covered slopes and wind ravaged gorse clumps with their candle flame flowers alight throughout the year. We clamber through the bracken and along the cliff edge to a small cove. We are accompanied by the staccato stone chipping song of the stonechats which are a common feature of this area. The rosy-breasted black-capped male is a beautiful sight as the sun catches his plumage while he sits atop a gorse bush or foxglove stem.

We cross a small stream and follow a path hugging a dry stone wall, trying not to lose our balance down the steep slope and with a strong March wind buffeting us. The path then evens out and we walk through stunted blackthorn which cling to the slope until the sheer cliff makes it impossible.

It was in one of these blackthorn bushes only a month earlier where I flushed a merlin which had left the bare high ground of its breeding site to feed on the more abundant bird life on the coast. The blackthorns are no more than shoulder high but that doesn't put crows off nesting in some of them.

We arrive at the cove and on the far face just above a small cave we are surprised to see three shags sitting on virtually completed nests. On the higher ledges three fulmars sit defiantly on their nesting ledges, but it is probably still too early in the season for them to have eggs.

Continuing around the cove the honking of two ravens in the sky above tells us that they probably have a nest too. We soon spot the bulky collection of large sticks, straggling down from a ledge, half hidden by an overhang.

Whilst we are pleased to see these birds we are still on the lookout for our chief target, the chough. The search for the chough is made much more tantalising by the ubiquitous presence of crows, jackdaws and ravens, all of which are black and at a casual glance in the distance could be choughs. Their characteristic orange curved beak and orange legs are not easily visible from far off. Although as I mentioned, they are not shy birds, they often just sit on the cliffs or forage inconspicuously among the tufts of thrift and stonecrop for insects and can easily pass unnoticed.

Today we are lucky. Two black birds with deep fingered wings come flying towards us from the hill behind.

They toss and frolic in the wind like large black butterflies, then surge forward with wings drawn close in to their bodies.

Peregrine Falcon

The tell-tale thin needle-like bill is also discernable though at first there is no noticeable colour. Then as they come close we can

observe their orange beaks and glossy plumage. They are immediately joined by another pair and as a final confirmation of their identity they give a series of long drawn 'chow' calls, carrying far, even in the wind.

There is one crevice which looks very suitable for a chough's nest and we scan that and the rest of the cliff face with anticipation, pinning our hopes on this because other likely places will be out of view. While we search with our binoculars there is more than a little disappointment when two jackdaws fly onto a ledge below us and into the very hole we had secretly 'earmarked' for the choughs. Our birds choose to fly further up the coast and land in a spot with thick vegetation where it is impossible to follow them. Watching from below is out of the question because even at low tide there is no exposed beach and the cliffs are steep.

In May we return again to the same spot hoping for more views of these rare birds. The ravens have now gone from their nest and the shags have been replaced by about 25 pairs of cormorants which have taken up their usual stations on a high section of the cliffs. They fly back and forth on regular fishing expeditions.

Behind the cove is a large slope of gorse and bracken which seems essential habitat for the feeding requirements of choughs.

Soon the birds come into view, heading towards us from the hill top. There are now five altogether and three of them swung round the promontary and disappeared out of sight, where we suspected there was a nest in some inaccessible crevice above the waves. We still had a dogged hope that our old crevice would turn up trumps and then sure enough we were overjoyed to see both male and female enter the place where only two months ago the jackdaws had been in occupation. As we sat on the cliff top and watched they entered the crevice 13 times within half an hour, giving us excellent views.

Since that year we have encountered other choughs. One pair was breeding close to a caravan park and the nest could be seen easily whilst walking along the shingle beach below. The bird refused to be disturbed from its nest despite a continuous procession of holiday makers wandering past or sitting nearby, oblivious of the chough's proximity.

We know of several inland eyries but a good coastal walk where there are high cliffs is as good a way as any of finding peregrines. One such walk is along a path which follows the contour of the cliff top and passes sometimes close to the sheer face, where below the pounding waves of the high tide are thrown back in fountains of spume and spray. A little further out in the waves the sleek glistening heads of grey seals can be seen before they roll effortlessly over and dive again for fish. Sometimes there are small groups of dolphins whose black dorsal fins appear and disappear as they play in the water.

Half way along the cliff walk where I knew there was an eyrie the previous year I scan the ledges and crevices with my binoculars. Eventually merging with the grey mottled rock I see the female, sitting immobile on her accustomed ledge. My friend whose binoculars are less powerful than mine is still doubtful. As we move closer we can clearly see her dark moustache and deadly sharp beak, but still there is no movement. At last she develops an instinctive sense of unease and shuffles back deeper into the recess. Only then can we see why she has clung so tenaciously to her ledge. We can just make out two eyasses (young peregrines) behind her. Not wishing to disturb her we move on, soon to be accompanied by the male patrolling the cliffs. He rattles out his distinctive alarm note, flying first out to sea and then back, following our course along the cliff until we are safely out of range.

To watch a pair of peregrines hunting, dive bombing out of the heavens at incredible speed and catching their prey on the wing is to observe aerial mastery at its best. The speed may seem slow at first, rapidly gaining pace as the bird slips sideways, scything through the air at an ever increasing angle of descent. In the early breeding season the male will often bring in his prey, a pigeon or a gull, and drop it to the female who catches it in the air, flying below him.

An unusual characteristic of this coastline is its cliff-nesting oyster catchers. They would normally lay their eggs amongst the shingle on the shore, but because it is here too narrow and subject to the tides they are unable to find suitable shore sites. They nest three to six metres up amongst the thrift and scree.

We returned home along the beach, quickly leaving a worried oyster catcher, doing its best to look unconcerned, to return to its cliff nest. One or two curlew probing with their long curved beaks among the seaweed are all we can see, apart from three mergansers floating off the shore. To cap an interesting morning we finished by watching a pair of rock pipits feeding almost fledged young in a little crack in the rock face barely a metre above the shore line.

Chough

MARSH AND ESTUARY
(including lowland lakes)

For our purposes, estuary in this part of the country usually means the **Dyfi**, although the picturesque **Afon Mawddach estuary** to the north has similar breeding species such as shelduck, redshank, oyster-catcher, ringed plover and merganser, some of which are also found along the low coast between the two estuaries. The Teifi estuary, just off our map to the south also has breeding shelduck, and **Cardigan Island** out in the bay has a thriving colony of lesser black-backed gulls.

Although the claims for the Dyfi are modest compared to the Wash or the Ribble in Lancashire, it does attract a number of interesting birds being the only extensive estuarine area between north and south Wales, along a coastline which for the most part is rocky. For those in the area it is the ideal place to see wintering wildfowl and migrating waders.

The R.S.P.B. reserve at **Ynyshir** takes in a large stretch of the marsh and mud flats of the estuary and from its comfortably constructed wooden hides you can obtain excellent views of the birds. Incidentally, the reserve contains woodland and moorland heath as well with such species as woodcock, lesser spotted woodpecker and one or two pairs of nightjar although these interesting birds are virtually non-existent in mid Wales and are probably already lost from the reserve.

It is an uplifting experience to be walking past gently swaying reed beds along the edges of the flats on a bright, crisp winter's morning with the sky blue and clear.

Overhead you can hear the throbbing of powerful wings as the white fronted geese circle and settle in one of the waterlogged fields. Up to a hundred winter here regularly. Flocks of wigeon, teal and mallard twist and turn over the river, their plumage shining in full colour as they catch the sun.

On the waters of the estuary mergansers, pintail and scoters are among the most frequent wildfowl to be seen. There are wintering

heron

golden plover, knot, dunlin, bar-tailed godwit and flocks of lapwings.

The flood-water pools in the fields are mirrors to the sky and curlews poke their long curved beaks in their own reflections, while the sheep graze placidly alongside.

Apart from the birds mentioned above, on any winter's day, or during migration, along this estuary you stand a chance of seeing the occasional rarity or chance visitor.

In the past twenty years such vagrants as the buff-breasted sandpiper, lesser yellow legs, spotted sandpiper, sabines gull, white-winged black tern and rock thrush have all been recorded here and a wide range of commoner birds, but ones rarely encountered at other places along the coast are seen regularly.

The attraction of the **Mawddach** and **Dysynni/Broadwater** estuaries, however, cannot be underrated: velvet scoter, pink-footed geese, long-tailed duck, curlew sandpiper, little gull, great and arctic skuas, iceland and glaucous gulls, lapland bunting and osprey are just a few of the species which are sometimes or regularly seen here.

In this book we are primarily concerned with the breeding birds, and on the Dyfi you can encounter some notable, if not exceptionable species.

In summer redshank and shelduck nest on the salt marshes and the former's constant piping call is a friendly accompaniment to a stroll next to the flats. There are also numbers of breeding lapwing. The latter would not have merited a mention in the past but in recent years, due to intensive farming, they have become scarce in many farmland areas. In mid Wales the lapwing is decidedly local, being found usually in river valleys, marshland or wet areas of the moors.

In 1985 there was a colony of black headed gulls nesting on the mud but these had gone by the following year.

Mergansers are one of the familiar birds of the estuary but they nest mostly higher up the river. This is the most southerly nesting place for this species in Britain (but see *'in search of sawbills'*, section 5).

The marshy hinterland with its extensive carpeting of heather known as **Borth Bog** or to give it its Welsh name, **Cors Fochno**, has snipe and curlew breeding. Sedge warblers and grasshopper warblers are here too and can always be heard calling in late spring or early summer.

In recent years a few pairs of reed warbler have bred at Ynyshir and its nearby marshes.

Water rail have bred and possibly the spotted crake too, but birds you might expect to be common like the moorhen or little grebe are quite scarce. This holds true in fact for much of mid Wales where these two species and others, like the reed bunting, a familiar sight in almost any English reedbed, are nowhere near as common.

Further inland there are many marshy fields but the largest marshland of all is **Tregaron Bog** also known as **Cors Caron**. Formerly red and black grouse could be found here and although the former may still breed in very small numbers, they have virtually disappeared. Dunlin also once bred on the marsh and at times, also the montagu's harrier.

Few birds can be called abundant on the bog although the whinchat is found in good numbers and there are a few stonechats. A walk along the former railway track will yield breeding snipe, curlew and grasshopper warblers. Near the river Teifi which runs through the centre of the bog there are a few pairs of redshank.

Breeding wildfowl are sparse, though shoveler and garganey have bred in the past, and the secretive water rail is no doubt a regular breeder. There are about 20 pairs of teal.

All in all, for the birdwatcher, Tregaron Bog is too often a disappointment despite its promise. Its vast desolate expanse always has an air of expectancy about it, as if its secret only needs to be unlocked.

As some compensation, both kite and buzzard frequently hunt over the marsh and there is a good chance of seeing a hen harrier in winter.

A large section of Tregaron Bog is in the hands of the Nature Conservancy Council. Birds are by no means the only wildlife of interest. The bog is for example the most southerly haunt of the large heath butterfly in Britain. The area is, however, of most importance for its botanical interest.

Other marshes in the area are smaller but nevertheless those near **Bethania** and **Trefenter** are quite expansive with numbers of whinchat, snipe, curlew and grasshopper warbler. Such places could well yield more exciting species given proper study.

The same sort of picture applies to the wetlands east of the **Cambrian mountains**, although low lying lakes have perhaps rather more resident grebes and swans and in some places the tufted duck or canada goose breed regularly. Such places include **Llan Bwch Llyn in Radnor**. **Rhosgoch Common** has a large colony of black-headed gulls and pre-1940 spotted crakes were recorded breeding on several occasions. Water rail may breed here and at **Newbridge Bog** regularly. **Montgomery** like Radnor also has a few tufted duck and rather more Canada Geese.

In the eastern extremities such as the **Teme Valley**, **Newtown** sewage works or near the **Wye** south of **Builth Wells** a few pairs of yellow wagtails may be found.

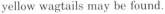

oystercatchers

FARM AND FIELD

If you take a walk along one of the many narrow country lanes in West Wales during the spring or summer you will be able to enjoy a tranquil outing with little harassment from noisy and smelly vehicles. On each side of you there will be steep grass verges, hedges with beech, hawthorn or hazel, with views of the Cambrian hills to the east. You will probably note that song birds are fewer than in corresponding lanes in lowland counties. Hole nesting species such as tits, treecreepers and nuthatches will be in good numbers but birds of the gardens, thickets and undergrowth will be fewer. All three woodpeckers are found though the greater spotted is the most numerous. Rarely will you see a wealth of blackbirds, thrushes, greenfinches, bulfinches and yellowhammers although robins, long tailed tits, mistle thrushes and of course the chaffinch will be as common as elsewhere. The comforting scenery and plentiful wild flowers will more than compensate for a thinner bird population.

Sometimes the only birds in sight will be members of the crow family. The carrion crow and magpie are especially common but rooks are not far behind especially near the coast and in river valleys. Between my home and Aberystwyth, eight miles away, there are as many as five rookeries.

Pied wagtails are usually to be seen flitting round the old farm buildings where they find plentiful insect life. Where there are groups of trees or small copses lining the streams or in the hollows, there will be jays, chiffchaffs and willow or marsh tits.

In the early mornings or at dusk you will hear the soft hooting of the tawny owls and occasionally the screech of the barn owl, or even see its ghost-like form silently floating over the hedges. Close to a campsite just outside Aberystwyth a pair of barn owls could be seen going in and out of a small stone barn and sailing eerily over the tents and barns in the half light, unbeknown to most of the campers in their makeshift homes below. They may well be still there although the drop in barn owl numbers nationally has been a concern of naturalists for many years.

Old stone barns and derelict buildings — testimony to the hardships of agricultural life — can be seen almost everywhere and, as a consolation, provide havens for a variety of birds. In one of such ruins we have seen a pied wagtail, house sparrow, redstart and swift fly into the holes and crevices one after the other, feeding their offspring. There are often jackdaw colonies in them too, their raucous chattering readily revealing their whereabouts. Pied flycatchers and tits may also make their homes in old walls and bridges.

Where there is rough pasture or boggy ground you may hear the drumming of the snipe or the fluting sounds of the curlew.

In the skies circling the distant hill tops or woods you will often see buzzards in the air. If you drive observantly it is a common sight to see these big brown, mottled birds sitting on telegraph poles or fence posts at the roadside and if you stop, they will slowly lumber off to a more distant outlook. Some will make their homes in the woods, but others will be contented to choose a site in a hedgerow tree after the fashion of the crows.

Ravens too can be heard, giving their throaty calls as they fly over. Although plentiful you will see the sparrow hawk less often, perhaps rushing along a hedgerow in pursuit of a small bird, or circling over its wood on an April morning.

little owl

Some birds have virtually disappeared from the farmland scene; the cirl bunting in the 1940's, the shrike, and more recently the woodlark in the early '70's. These days corncrakes are rarely heard in the fields and meadows, having suffered disastrously from modern farming techniques, yet they survived here longer than most other places in southern Britain.

Some facts may surprise the visitor from the city. The chaffinch is far commoner than the house sparrow whilst in West Wales at least the starling nesting in woodland or farmland is a notable rarity yet it is common enough in towns or in winter flocks. The kestrel, whilst inhabiting cliffs on the coast or inland, apparently rarely makes its nest in a tree. Most surprisingly, there are thousands of fields which look suitable for skylarks, but rarely will you see them except on the moors or near the coast. They don't seem to like re-seeded and fertilised meadows.

Birds like the hedgesparrow, wren and yellow hammer though common, are not found in the same abundance as in lowland counties. The song thrush and blackcap seem to shun higher woods (though the thrush is especially partial to rhododendron thickets) whereas their respective cousins the mistle thrush and garden warbler seem to have no such inhibitions. The greenfinch is only common in shrubby sheltered areas while the equally scarce bullfinch benefits from overgrown disused railway lines or bramble tangles in young plantations. The goldfinch thrives better and may well be the second most numerous finch in some of our districts.

There are several farmland species which are either absent or rare on the west side of the Cambrians, which are found, at least sparsely, in eastern mid Wales. Amongst these are the common partridge, tree sparrow, and lesser whitethroat. Like the bullfinch this latter species also seems to make use of disused railway embankments. A few pairs only are present in Ceredigion whilst the numerous common whitethroat is plentiful in coastal districts.

The little owl is another rarity in the west. In April 1986 I was pleasantly surprised to see one at **Capel Bangor** as I hadn't seen one in the area before. It is commoner further east and we have twice seen it near Welshpool: a greyish, sleepy round ball perched immobile on a telegraph pole. The more easily overlooked long-eared owl prefers conifer woodlands or thorn thickets where it encounters far less competition from its more powerful cousin the tawny owl, which is not unknown to kill this and other owls. The long-eared owl is rare but could be seen virtually anywhere; north **Carmarthen**, the **Radnor Forest** or by **Lake Vyrnwy** are some of the most likely areas.

There are other species represented perhaps by just the odd pair on the fringe of mid Wales such as the red legged partridge, turtle dove or the hawfinch. This elusive, dumpy finch with its bounding flight is often overlooked but is seen, for example, frequently in the vicinity of Newtown. These species are all more easily seen further east and will here more readily interest the local rather than the visiting bird watcher.

All of this may give you the impression that the farmland habitat has less to offer than others. Perhaps this simply reflects our emphasis in a book which is trying to convey the special attractions of mid Wales in contrast to other species which may be found more commonly in the English border counties.

The fact is that there are more than 60 species associated with farmland, with its hedgerows, fields, common land and villages. This variety is greater than for any other habitat in the region.

We now leave a habitat in which there are few typical species especially associated with mid Wales, to one in which there are a number of characteristic birds, though none of them are confined to Wales. Indeed some, like the goosander, are newcomers arriving only in the last decade or two.

Blue Tit
Coal Tit
Great Tit
Willow Tit

UPLAND LAKES AND RIVERS

Mid Wales abounds in rivers flowing through picturesque wooded valleys and they offer ideal habitats for watching some interesting species associated with fast running waters.

Sit by a riverbank with a picnic and one of our typical riverbirds should put in an appearance.

The elegant and colourful misnamed grey wagtails wagging their long tails as they stand on the stones protruding from the swirling waters are delightful to watch. So is the rotund little dipper with its white bib, probing among the rocks in mid stream, or zipping past like a bullet to land on a rock downstream. These birds unfortunately appear to be getting scarcer, possibly due to the effects of acid rain killing off the insects and crustacea on which they feed.

The common sandpiper, that dainty little wader, is fairly plentiful both at low and high altitudes, breeding by low-lying shingle-lined rivers or peat pools on the hills. It can be seen running up and down the water's edge nervously. Its piping call is easily recognised as is its characteristic, interrupted flight-bursts of rapid wing beats and gliding on bowed wings, allowing you to note its white wing bars as it skims the water, before landing again a few hundred metres further along the water's edge.

That other famous bird of the river, the irridescent blue-backed kingfisher, is rarely seen. It prefers the slow muddy waters of flatter country and I have only been lucky enough to see it twice in four years, once on the Ystwyth in September, and once on the Severn at Llanidloes. Herons often nest in tree colonies convenient for fishing on the rivers and sandmartins colonise riverbanks, boring their holes in banks, sometimes only a foot or so above the water.

All of these species I find close to my home near the **Ystwyth** and all are just as likely to be met with on other suitable waters in mid Wales.

In the trees along the riverbanks you can catch a glimpse of the orange-red flash of the redstart's tail, or watch the aptly named pied flycatcher with the male in contrasting black and white plumage searching for insects in an alder tree. Unlike his relative the spotted flycatcher he is less inclined to fly out after an insect and return repeatedly to the same branch. These and others, like the marsh and willow tit, and pied wagtail, are attracted to the vicinity of water.

It must be admitted, that although Wales boasts many upland lakes, reservoirs and pools, they are not noted for their wealth and variety of bird life. Mallard, the commonest breeding duck on the rivers as well as the lakes, are plentiful enough while the teal breeds in small numbers around the pools and upland bogs. It was in one such place that I found a nest in 1985. It was high up on the moor, near a small stream which looped its way through the short tussock grass, a short distance from a peaty pool. I accidentally flushed the female from her nest in a clump of grass close to the stream where she was sitting on nine creamy coloured eggs. The nest of this species is not easy to find partly because its catholic choice of site, often well away from water, gives almost unlimited scope.

Some of the larger lakes now have goosanders which may be looked for on Llyn Brianne, the **Elan Valley** Lakes and Llyn Clywedog and **Lake Vyrnwy**, both in Montgomery. The latter lake which forms part of a large R.S.P.B. nature reserve (in association

Female Goosander in nesting hole

25

with landowners and the water authorities) also has resident great crested grebes and tufted duck on occasions.

The upland pools sometimes hold colonies of black-headed gulls which may range from a couple of pairs up to two hundred or more. The largest I know in Ceridigion is currently on **LLyn Syfydrin** where around 250 pairs nest mostly on the island in the middle of the lake. If you approach anywhere near the lake the resulting cacophony of their outraged voices is a shock in this otherwise quiet place.

This lake, and other upland lakes will usually have pochard, golden eye and maybe a few whooper swans in winter. Some waters will have only a pair or two of coot breeding on them whilst the moorhen has no taste at all for acidic lakes and surging rivers. This species so common on English ponds is curiously scarce in mid Wales hiding away for the most part in slow running dykes and channels at lower altitudes.

Dipper

In search of Sawbills

Looking for sawbills in summer would have been a pointless exercise in mid Wales 40 years ago. The red breasted merganser spread from the north reaching first **Merioneth** and then the Ceredigion shores of the Dyfi in 1969. There its expansion southwards had temporarily come to a halt, at least until 1985 when we proved breeding on the Ystwyth.

Thirty years ago both the merganser and goosander were winter visitors. The former species was joined by its larger relative in 1970 when the first Welsh goosander was found breeding in Radnor. Its preference is for inland situations whereas the merganser nests and often feeds close to the sea. The goosander is spreading and apart from the upland lakes mentioned on p 25 it is breeding on such rivers as the **Tywi**, **Cothi** and **Teifi** in north Carmarthenshire, Vyrnwy and Severn in Montgomery, and Wye in Radnor. Just recently it has started to establish itself on the Rheidol and Ystwyth rivers in north Ceredigion.

Our study of the Ystwyth mergansers in 1986 began with the sighting of a pair two miles up river from the sea in April and a few weeks later in mid May, the same or a second pair were seen about six miles further upstream.

Apart from birds on the sea, a common enough sight in spring, nothing more was seen until I observed two females swimming close to the river bank on a warm June evening. I watched them swimming for a short while until they suddenly rose from the water and flew upstream and out of sight.

This excited me so much that I returned to the same spot the next afternoon but approached from the opposite direction after wading across the clear shallow waters of the river.

This time I was with a friend, and we made our way cautiously along the river bank, through the gorse and broom scrub, now aflame with their bright yellow flowers. Where the vegetation was too thick, we walked on the shingle lining the river banks.

We then sat down on a section of the river bank which gave us a clear view of a long stretch of water and waited. Very soon we were rewarded with the sight of two females in the company of one male, flying up river towards us. The birds passed with a swish of wings and were gone from sight.

We remained where we were hoping to see the birds return. The sun was already low on the horizon and its red light set the bracken covered hills alight, turning them into a raging russet orange colour which was reflected in the fast flowing river like licking flames. We were about to 'break camp' when the three birds reappeared again, this time flying downstream and disappearing around a bend in the river.

Evening was obviously a good time to watch these mergansers and we returned around 6pm the following day since this seemed a time when they liked to feed, and hoped, that like humans, they were creatures of regular habit. Sure enough, almost to the minute the male merganser appeared swimming in mid-stream, looking alertly around is if he expected something to happen. A minute or two later with a flurry of wings the two females swooped down onto the water and skidded to a halt alongside him. They had certainly come direct from the vegetation above the river bank and we immediately suspected they had clutches of eggs. Having established the almost certainty of breeding we decided prudently not to disturb the birds any more and leave them alone to their stretch of the river.

We did return, out of curiosity, three weeks later and were overjoyed to see the rusty-headed female paddling forcefully downstream, trailed by a convoy of seven similar-looking ducklings.

Although the male goosander can be very conspicious in his black and white plumage, he and his blue-grey plumaged mate with her red head, can be very elusive. I saw a pair on the Ystwyth on the 1st of May 1984 but repeated follow up visits all drew blanks. The same applied with efforts to relocate a pair seen on **Llyn Frongoch**, and more exciting still, a pair flushed near **Parsons Bridge** on the **Rheidol River** as they swam close to the cover of steep rocks. Admittedly we saw males on the Cothi and near **Beulah (Breconshire)** and a female on the Tywi on round tour car drives but locating resident goosanders which we could study locally was another matter. No breeding was confirmed in Ceredigion until 1985 when an observer saw a female with a duckling on the Rheidol.

We had made some effort to locate goosanders in this area ourselves that March.

After parking the car off the road near a small church, I walked along a footpath, along the dry stone walls bordering the fields now glistening with young barley. As we neared the river its rushing sound reverberated from below. Here the river has cut a deep and narrow gorge in the rock and its steep sides are thick with oak and birch, their trunks densely coated with moss and lichen. Clambering down the small shale strewn path was like wandering through an enchanted wood.

This part of the river Rheidol is perhaps one of the most romantic of the area. The trees almost completely screen the river from view, only its gushing reveals its presence as it cascades, twists and rushes through the narrow fissures of steep overhanging rocks or over large boulders, forming deep, brown pools in small inlets. It could be a corner of the garden of Eden, so virgin and undisturbed it appears, so wild and free.

The overhanging tree roots and the holes in the rocks would provide ideal nesting sites for goosanders although they more often choose holes in tree trunks.

The ruins of old lead mines, perched above the river, add their aura of unreality to the scene.

From the high banks you can look down and watch the dippers plunging into the fast flowing currents in their search for small crustacea and then re-emerge, the water pearling from their slate coloured backs. Then they bob up and down nervously before shooting off like bullets to another feeding spot.

A pair of grey wagtails pirouette over the water, catching insects and then settling on the boulders, their long tails undulating as if on a spring. So attractive as these small birds are they are not what we were looking for that day.

I began to think my imagination and optimism were getting the better of me when we rounded a sharp bend in the river and there

Goosander pair

below us, in a sudden flash of black and white, a pristine pair of goosanders rose from the water and flew off through the trees. We couldn't believe our luck.

The following season we saw a few goosanders but none so likely as this pair, but in 1987 we had more good fortune, this time patrolling the Ystwyth as part of the British Trust for Ornithology's survey of this species.

Again it was in March, but this time we were in the neighbourhood of what used to be Hafod, a mansion now long disappeared leaving only legends, beautiful trees and grounds to posterity. We stood staring at the river looking intently at two birds on the water close to the bank. This was the first time we had seen a pair of goosanders on the Ystwyth for nearly three years, but to our disappointment they drifted slowly out of sight downstream.

The next day, at the end of a two mile walk, dodging among the pines by the river and feeling frustrated at our failure to see anything, suddenly the pair flew from the river in front of us.

Two weeks later, and we saw another pair three miles down river, flying rapidly towards us and then past, and out of sight round a bend of the river. There were many spruce trees here as at the last site but also oaks and birches flanking the river.

I trudged, excited and hopeful along steep banks carpeted with heather and bilberry, and over steep rocks looking for signs of these elusive birds. It was only the next day but I was impatient for further clues. I had just reached the head of a gorge where further exploration, I knew, would be impossible, when there in a deep, still pool beneath steepsided rocks drifted a lovely male goosander. I retreated out of sight and took up a position several hundred yards downstream partially hidden in the trees.

Patiently I waited for what seemed like an eternity but was probably little over an hour, and then the goosander appeared on the water about 60 yards from where I sat. Suddenly, reminiscent of the mergansers, the female suddenly appeared beside him, head feathers raised as though suddenly braking hard as it landed on the rippling waters. After a few seconds both birds flew off.

Not far from here a few days later we made a surprising discovery. A tawny owl incubating one egg of its own and two goosander's eggs in a riverside oak. It seems the goosanders had laid first and had been dispossessed by this strongest of our resident owls. More hopefully, though, the sawbills had from the evidence at least managed to find a new home of their own.

Nest boxes suitable for goosanders may be the answer since suitable tree holes are at a premium. They have for example, been used successfully to tempt goosanders at Lake Vyrnwy but it appears to be doing very well on its own at the moment with already well over a hundred pairs in Wales.

Although more of a long shot, perhaps, nest boxes could be used to entice golden eye to stay beyond April to breed on our upland Welsh lakes or rivers where they are common enough in early Spring. There are now more than 30 pairs breeding in Scotland, making their homes primarily in well placed nesting boxes.

In 1987 I saw a single female in suitable habitat on the upper Rheidol in March, and observed a male chasing a group of three females on Llyn Brianne, so perhaps one day we might be able to add another hole nesting duck to our list of breeding birds of mid Wales.

Merganser pair

goldfinch
redpoll

THE VALLEY AND UPLAND WOODS

These are the areas where Wales comes into its own. There is hardly another place in the whole of Britain boasting such stretches of unspoilt wooded valleys with their chortling streams and their soft wild beauty.

The woodlands are plentiful and range from the coast up to 300 metres elevation or more. The classic habitat is, of course, the hanging oak woods although there are also fine stands of beech and, on the boggier ground, willow, birch and alder. The sessile oak is dominant on the steep slopes clinging tenaciously to the thin soils, whereas the larger common oak replaces it lower down the hillsides where the soil is better.

These woodlands are home to many species which are perhaps commoner here than in most places in these islands. Birds like the common redstart which also likes more open places with old stone walls, stone barns and derelict buildings with perhaps rowans and hawthorns dotted about. The leaf carpeted slopes of oak and beech woods with scant undergrowth very much suit the needs of the woodwarbler whose rising mellifluous warbling can be heard all around in springtime. You will also hear the piercing trill of the nuthatch, and see the treecreeper busily spiralling up decaying tree trunks in search of insects.

Indeed hole nesting species are generally well represented in these woods. Tits are abundant, tawny owls and great spotted woodpeckers are common, though green and lesser spotted wood-peckers are scarcer. Woodcock are found in damper places to the east of the mountains, but are much scarcer in the west.

Perhaps the most notable bird of these Welsh woodlands however is the pied flycatcher. This lovely little black and white bird, or in the case of the female a rather more sombre brown and white, breeds in holes in trees, stone walls or even in bridges and buildings. In some woods, such as those on the mountain road from **Rhayader** to Aberystwyth they are virtually the dominant species in summer,

31

Pied Flycatcher

being about as numerous as the bluetit and chaffinch. The extensive use of nest boxes has enabled this species to increase both its range and numbers. In the woods around the R.S.P.B. reserve at **Gwenffrwd**, 330 pairs bred in the season of 1983. Over 60 pairs nest annually on their reserve at Ynyshir, whilst 130 pairs were reported breeding at Lake Vyrnwy Reserve in 1984 of which 104 chose nest boxes. These figures at reserves spaced as much as 50 miles apart indicate the strength of the pied flycatcher in mid Wales.

Where the ground is a little more open, the tree pipit is another very familiar species, parachuting down from the skies onto the ground or the tops of trees.

The raven, like the buzzard, is found in most of our habitats described in this book, and makes its nest in oaks as well as pines in the valley woods.

It is the majestic buzzard though which lays claim to be lord of the woodlands. It is the commonest raptor, easily outnumbering the more wary sparrowhawk which is second, and indeed it is perhaps more numerous here than anywhere else in Britain. You may go into the hill country on a clear October day and see ten or twelve or even more buzzards in a single morning.

In spring it is an ever present sight, flapping leisurely between the trees, or more often, soaring overhead with its curved wing-tips, mewing its shrill cry. You can often see several in the air at once, particularly in fine weather.

buzzard   Even when there are no buzzards in sight a bird will reveal its

presence with mewing calls from the depths of a wood.

The relationship between buzzard and crow is fascinating. Low flying birds over farmland are rarely without the constant attention of harrying crows, which are not only disturbed by the presence of buzzards in their territory in the breeding season, but also at other times of the year.

In *The Birds of Cardiganshire* (1967) by Morrey-Salmon, Ingram and Condry, the authors quote the buzzard's diet as including carrion crows and magpies. We have personally witnessed an incident of a buzzard at a freshly killed carcase of a crow and found other crows dead in old nests which we thought were probably victims of the buzzard.

In Search of the Kite

If the buzzard is lord of the woods, though, it is the red kite which is the real star of the region, confined as it is since the turn of the century to mid Wales.

In previous centuries it was a common scavenging bird of English towns, country villages and lowland woods. By the end of the 19th century it was already extinct in all of Britain except the upper Tywi district, where it was thought only five or six birds survived, and possibly the odd bird or two elsewhere.

A local naturalist of the early part of this century, Professor J.H. Salter with University College of Wales, Aberystwyth, played an important part in assisting the kite's survival in mid Wales. Numbers fluctuated but remained perilously low until the fifties when its population, despite only mediocre breeding success, steadily increased.

The predation of egg collectors has recently presented a serious threat to its recovery, with seven or eight nests robbed in 1985 and again in 1986, even with the increased vigilance and protection afforded by the relevant organisations. Nevertheless in 1987 of 43 breeding pairs, 39 young were reared successfully and that is a record this century. In 1988 47 pairs reared 38 young.

The kite breeds on both sides of the Cambrian mountains making a scrappy, untidy large nest of sticks, mud and oddments, usually in a tall beech or oak, but sometimes in smaller trees such as alder, where I recently saw one from the car no more than six metres above the ground. Unfortunately I later heard from the farmer that it had been robbed of its three eggs by a predator, probably a crow, just when it was near the point of hatching. We have, of course, as should be the case of all people not directly concerned with their protection, never approached an occupied nest. One old nest I knew was several metres high in a beech as though it had been used year after year, like an eagle or osprey. Unfortunately this magnificent beech tree was recently cut down, illustrating the need for care in protecting the kite's favoured haunts.

Although it is often very conspicuous floating serenely over roads or hilltops within easy view of motorists, or circling above the

Kite
at nest

delighted birdwatcher, who has come to see this species above all
other, it is easily overlooked. One couple I met had spent a week
looking with kites under their noses — or rather over their heads,
without seeing a single bird. To be fair, I think they must have been
very unlucky as well as none too observant.

Kites are usually seen in similar places to the buzzards; circling the thermals over the hill tops, beating along the edge of woodland or methodically hunting over the sheep walks looking for carrion or rodents.

The kite is an impressive bird on the wing and its five foot wing span exceeds that of the buzzard. It's appearance is more rakish with a slimmer body, longer narrower wings and a longer tail which is noticeable even when the characteristic fork is not.

The buzzard's wings are straighter and appear broadly striped with brown and cream although some birds are much paler or darker than average. Where the buzzard's plumage altogether gives the appearance of being uniformly mottled, the kite appears to be patchy. If you are lucky enough to see it from above, from the top of a hill or roadside above the valley, or with the low light of the setting sun catching its plumage, then its whitish head and rufous red tail will be seen in all its glory. From below the large white patches and blackish areas on the wings are prominent and the tail can appear almost orange. The overall impression is of a bird patterned in black, white and rufous red.

On a recent drive from Aberystwyth to **Llanidloes** in late March I was able to watch three buzzards and two kites circling tightly overhead with their differing wing patterns transparently clear in the spring sunshine. On other occasions we have watched these two large raptors soaring with the smaller sparrow hawk, and on another with a peregrine in attendance. Most exciting of all for me, was one occasion in March when I watched no less than ten kites milling around a valley prior to dispersing to their nesting woods.

Virtually all the Welsh kites are to be found within the area of our map. Places close to the upper Tywi, Rheidol or Ystwyth are as good places as any to see the kite, but please don't linger, and even more important don't enter any woodlands where the kite may be nesting between March and June. It can be readily seen at any time of the year, although there is a partial migration south in autumn. Personally I find the kite is less easy to come across during the May to July period.

Recently I saw a goshawk circling over one of our valley deciduous woods. At first it might have been a slightly small buzzard but the tail was too long. Kite, I thought, but then the thought was rejected almost as soon as it was conceived. The wings were too compact and the tail flat-ended, as it soared closer, now looking like a huge sparrow hawk.

Both of these birds have the typical accipiter hawk shape with broad wings (which can look pointed) and relatively long tails. The sparrowhawk is nearer kestrel size (the female is, however, much bigger than the male which is a little smaller than the kestrel), whereas the goshawk has a bulk and wing span almost equalling that of a buzzard. In good light the very pale undertail coverts are also a distinguishing feature.

In the next section we will refer to this exciting new species again which, with its smaller relative the sparrow hawk, the kite and the buzzard, provide an exciting array of predators which can be looked for in the upland woods and valleys.

BIRDS OF THE CONIFER PLANTATIONS

Siskin
above

Kites
left

The much criticised spruce, fir and larch plantations are a mixed blessing. They are planted so closely together that once they attain sapling height the sunlight to the undergrowth is cut off and it dies. Often in this state they hold little more than wood pigeons, magpies, jays, goldcrests, coaltits and the ubiquitous chaffinch. A walk through them is often like a walk through a cemetery. The thick hanging skirts of the pendulent branches of the trees at the edges prevent views of the interior, and a dark impenetrable silence envelops them; only the crunch of one's own footsteps echoes back.

There is concern over the invasion of the 'evergreen jungle' swallowing our moors and destroying its wild life, aiding the leaching of aluminium into fresh water, poisoning it and spoiling the landscape with its dreary monotony.

There is, however, another side to the story: When the plantations are young they attract tree pipits, whitethroats, willow warblers and other songsters. They provide suitable hunting grounds and nesting sites for the short-eared owl and hen harrier although in Wales the latter is found less on plantations than elsewhere in northern England or Scotland. The plantations have also benefitted that other exciting species, the black grouse, at least in the short term. When the forests are cut down there could be opportunities for other birds, the nightjar for instance, which might find this new 'heathland' to its liking.

There are other interesting newcomers to these evergreen forests. One of the most familiar is the siskin. This attractive little green and yellow finch spread during the seventies and eighties from the north into the fir plantations of mid Wales and is now breeding widely, if thinly, in many areas.

In 1985 a drive along the **Tregaron** mountain road revealed the little siskin breeding in the fir plantations there in small groups of up to half a dozen pairs. They were accompanied by much larger numbers of redpolls which seemed unusually common that year. The

37

following year we saw fewer siskins near the mountains, but three pairs which had used our neighbour's bird table for several weeks, stayed to breed close to my home. Incidentally despite their small size the siskins were quite capable of forcing both blue tits and great tits to take their places behind them at the nutbag. These birds appeared in April and by early May it was clear from their distinctive call notes that they were going to breed close by. (If you plan to study siskins do learn to recognise their plaintive call notes.) It is now well established and in springtime these dainty finches can be seen flying overhead in pairs to their tiny, almost invisible nests in the top, slender branches of the firs.

The crossbill is another recent coloniser of the mature spruce forests, though in fewer numbers than the siskin. Both species are also winter visitors. The rose-red male crossbill is a really attractive bird if you can catch a glimpse of him, quite often sitting in a prominent position in the crowns of spruce or pine. His mate is greener, rather like a streaky greenfinch with a larger head and parrot-like crossed-over beak mandibles.

The plantations are vast and the birds can be very elusive but look for them where the trees are taller with clusters of pendulent cones. Small, dense-growing conifer thickets are of no use. They breed very early in the year but are seen most readily from June to October: they bound overhead in small flocks drawing your attention with their characteristic loud chip, chip, chip call, interspersed with short trills and rattling notes as they settle on their favoured trees. It is fascinating to see them grappling with cones larger than themselves, extracting the succulent seeds with consummate skill, using their perfectly adapted crossed mandibles.

On crisp and bright February mornings we have observed several, including a polygamous male with two females, flying to and fro from their feeding trees to their nests. In 1988 we noted several other pairs in north Ceredigion although intermittent breeding has only been proven since 1977. In Montgomery several pairs often nest at **Lake Vyrnwy** and some in the **Dyfnant** and **Hafren Forests**. In south Merioneth birds can be seen regularly in the **Dyfi Forest** and the species is also found in **Radnor Forest**.

In **Brecon** the crossbill is found in the northern conifer woods.

The third small newcomer to the fir conifer plantation is in many ways the most surprising; the firecrest! Until the late 1960's it was confined to the New Forest area in Hampshire, then it spread dramatically with scores of pairs in just one wood in Buckinghamshire in the early 1970's. So far as mid Wales is concerned there were 6 pairs of firecrests at Lake Vyrnwy in 1982 and four pairs produced 14 young. Other pairs have nested and still breed in mid Wales though the future for this tiny bird is still by no means settled as numbers fluctuate throughout England and Wales.

The seventh rare and exciting new species — there is something to be said for these forests after all — is the goshawk, whose return to regular breeding in Britain is thanks to a combination of falconers' releases, part deliberate, and part accidental, the growth of the timber industry and perhaps a new attitude to birds of prey. The goshawk is at home in large open woodland of all kinds — deciduous, conifer or mixed. Like the sparrowhawk it flies low amongst the

Crossbill   trees, remaining amazingly undetected for so large a bird (as with other bird-preying species the female is much larger than the male). We were thrilled to be able to locate a pair in a northern mountainous forest which first drew our attention by emitting screaming calls from the depth of the wood. A few days later, sitting in a quiet spot, high up overlooking the wood we waited to see if we could catch a glimpse of these secretive birds. The alarm calls of a mistle thrush made us attentive and then we saw it: a medium-sized hawk with grey-brown wings and characteristic dazzling white under-tail coverts, splayed out, so that even from above they were clearly visible as stripes either side of the tail. The bird flew off, out of sight behind the firs. A short time later we again watched for the birds and for several minutes were able to observe the male hunting along the slopes or circling the hill top in the company of a buzzard. This time we waited, concealed from view, and were rewarded an hour later by the male goshawk reappearing, gathering pace as it zoomed below us, almost brushing the tree tops, veering to one side and flying up one of the rides between the trees. Here it was joined by the female, which rose from the wood, climbed for height and began circling with her mate. What an exciting discovery this was. We can only hope that these hawks will have continued success throughout Wales.

The relationship between the conifer plantations and birds like the hen harrier and short-eared owl has already been referred to. There used to be about 20 pairs of hen harriers breeding in northern Wales, including a number in Montgomery. Unfortunately in 1985 breeding success was catastrophic with only one of fourteen pairs rearing young. The following year saw a slight improvement but it is still worrying. Up until now no reason for this failure has been advanced but investigations being carried out by the RSPB and other organisations are very important in seeking to find the causes and remedy them. Similar research is being carried out into the drop in numbers of dippers, ring ouzels and dunlin. We refer later to the connection between pesticides and infertility in raptors, a situation which has happily been corrected.

The short eared owl is a variable resident, depending on the supply of voles and suitable territory which, as we have suggested, rapidly alters as the young conifers grow. These owls, which at first sight look more like small buzzards or harriers than owls, as they quarter the moors and plantations, currently breed in the Eppynt Forest south of Builth Wells, in parts of Montgomery and occasionally on the mid Cambrians.

In search of the Black Grouse

As with the harrier and short eared owl, we are including the black grouse in this section although, like them, arguably, it more rightly belongs to the birds of the moors. Its favourite territory lies at the interface between upland moor and young fir plantation with a mixture of other young trees as well.

It feeds on heather and bilberry as well as young birch and fir shoots and is therefore most likely to be found where a combination of these plants grow.

Black grouse are very thinly distributed and are easily over-looked, being active primarily in the early mornings or evenings, but it is worth making the effort to find these handsome birds. Since the last war the species has increased notably in Wales although the leks, or meeting grounds where the males display to the females, are only attended by a few birds. Of a study of sites in Wales, in fact, half of the leks had one male bird present only.

In mid Wales black grouse are most often seen at such places as the Dyfnant Forest north of Machynlleth, Foel Friog, Lake

Vyrnwy, Llangynog all in Montgomery; **Ffarmers** in Carmarthen,**Llanddewi Brefi** and **Anglers Retreat** in Ceredigion and several places in north Brecon.

In Ceredigion we have made several forays into the hills looking for black grouse. Knowing of their presence I drove along a mountain track high in the hills near **Nant-y-moch**. It was about 6.00 in the morning and the mist had still not lifted, but the sun was managing to break through and turn the dew soaked grass into a sea of glistening pearls. Through the cool and quiet morning air we caught the low bubbling sound of the blackcock at its lek. We looked at the scene and wondered if the birds could really be here because many of the pines were already 2 metres high or more. Nevertheless there were still quite large patches of heather and bilberry and the bubbling continued to reassure any doubts I might have entertained about their presence.

Then, out of the blue, a blackcock rose up in front of us and whirred away, skimming the crowns of the firs. Shortly afterwards, another flew up a hundred metres away. Then there was silence. I looked at my watch. It was 6.50am. Had we arrived at 7.00 o'clock we would have heard and seen nothing.

This experience whetted our appetite to have another go for the black grouse but this time we would try our own place, a habitat that looked just right not far from Strata Florida near Tregaron.

It was November and the weather forecast was grim: gale force winds and heavy showers with snow on high ground. Not exactly the ideal conditions for a bird watching outing on the Welsh hills.

Black Grouse at Lek

It was only a short drive from **Llanilar**, through the wooded Ystwyth valley, up into the Forestry Commission plantations as far as we could go and then park the car. Above us was a lake of clear

blue sky but to the north and west threatening big black swirls of cloud hung over the foreheads of the hills.

We set off up the track which led through the young spruce and pine and out onto the bare hills. Half way up the track traversed a farm yard. The gaunt grey farm house stood silently looking out over the steep-sided valley.

Thick conifer plantations are never a favourite haunt of birds even in summer. Their hard needles provide little nourishment for insects, the staple diet of so many birds. In autumn, however, they become one vast cemetery of monumental silence. Only the rustling wind and gurgling rivulets provide an accompaniment to the scrape of our boots on the wet gravelly path.

Very occasionally a chaffinch, in a flash of white and brown, darts across our path or a fragile pipit soars upwards in a brave attempt to challenge the wind, only to be thrown mercilessly down the valley like a discarded autumn leaf.

After half an hour's climb we emerged from the plantations out onto the bare hillside. The wind is fiercer now but our halo of blue sky still hovers above us.

Suddenly, from a small stream a few yards in front of us a fat russet-brown bird shoots up, flies skimming over the tops of the saplings and drops like a stone; a solitary woodcock, probably resting. They are crepuscular birds and rarely seen on the wing unless at dawn or dusk.

We scan the surrounding hills with our binoculars. We are investigating the area for likely black grouse habitats. It is not a common bird in the area and the only reasonable chance of seeing any of them is to find suitable habitats and search them religiously, or undertake an early morning (or evening) vigil in spring to listen for the distinctive sounds of the lek.

There was no sign of any bird life at all. They were all probably cowering in the trees, conserving energy, apart from a small group of cavorting crows down in the valley.

The tiny white and grey stone farm houses nestle far below in the green undulations of the valley floor. Not another person is to be seen anywhere and you have a view of tens of miles. We clamber and stumble through the marshy waterlogged ground, tripping in old tractor furrows and up onto the higher dryer areas. Approaching the brow of a hill is always as exciting event, not knowing what view will confront you on the other side.

We battled the wind to reach the summit and were offered the whole expanse of soft flowing hills as far away as the Brecon Beacons. A smooth furrowed skin of greens and browns met our eyes as stabs of sunlight pierced the thick mantle of cloud. Below us now was what we were looking for: a beautiful slope of thick springy heather and bilberry, ideal for black grouse.

We split up and wandered down the slope hardly daring to hope we would see anything. The place looked just right but at times like this you need a bit of luck and grouse can often keep to cover.

We were almost at the foot of the slope and convinced we had drawn a blank when about 100 metres away two large velvety black birds with thin wing bars and a flash of white under the tail, whirred up into the sky. In the excitement I couldn't extricate my binoculars from inside my anorak but it was as if the birds knew this, for after reaching a good safe height, they turned, their wings glistening in the sunlight and flew back almost over our heads, dropping down out of sight. As we sprang down the remaining few metres of heather and bilberry, two ruddy brown females broke cover and flew off to join their mates.

Common
Sandpiper
calling

For us these sightings alone had made the whole day worthwhile.

THE HIGH GROUND

The high moorlands often seem bereft of birds or of any wildlife for that matter. The scouring winds, driving rain and careering clouds seem determined to keep all animal life out of their domain. Only the courageous little meadow pipit seems able to survive the buffeting. It flies up from the ground at regular intervals, emitting its high pitched peep-peep, and is carried off by the wind.

In brighter weather the pipit may be accompanied by the crystal clear fluting tones of the lark rising in the sky. The skylark is second only to the meadow pipit in numbers on these open moors.

The moors have a fascination, the wild hill tops beckon as though promising mystery and adventure. Even mile upon mile of weary empty trudging does not deter those smitten by the attraction of desolate places; and always something might just chance to turn up; a merlin flashing by a stream, a golden plover calling from a hill top.

We reach the moors through wooded valleys, beyond the scattered birch, willow or rowan trees laden with their red berries. The narrow roads take us past steep, rocky gorges or cliffs where the tumbling, somersaulting streams run downhill, close to the roadside. Here the whinchat is at home, perched on an old fence post or fern stem. It loves the tall grass, rough vegetation and bracken covered slopes. It belongs to that select group of summer visitors — redstart, pied flycatcher, wood warbler and tree pipit — for which mid Wales provides some of the best habitat in Britain and supports correspondingly high concentrations.

Another chat, the wheatear or white-arse as its name denotes, is also at home on the upper slopes, but in more barren areas where it flits from stone to stone revealing its white rump. In rocky places, with boulders or stone walls you will see many wheatears in summer, conspicuous in their grey, black and white colours clicking loudly from the rocks.

Overhead the bass croak of the ponderous raven will be heard even in autumn as it swoops over its crags, surprising you with

Raven on nest

sudden acrobatic feats. It lays its clutch of greenish-brown blotched eggs in its huge mound of sticks lined with sheep's wool as early as February, in defiance of wind and snow. At lower altitudes it habitually nests in conifer or oak woods but high in the hills it is in its true element, rolling and somersaulting, showing its characteristic wedged tail.

The raven probably survives better here than anywhere else in Britain, benefiting from the plentiful supply of carrion from dead sheep. I have often seen their nests on a crevice or rocky ledge above a canyon or stream, and it is not unusual to see a sheep's carcass not far from the nest, in the valley below.

Occasionally ravens will use a low stunted tree on the moor for their nests, if there is no other site available. We know of a pair on a windswept moor near **Pontrhydfendigaid**. Here there are no cliffs and not another tree for miles around so the birds have made their bulky nest in the fragile looking branches of the hawthorn, its stick structure decorated with macabre looking pieces of sheep skeleton.

If you are lucky you will also glimpse the magnificent peregrine falcon patrolling the cliffs, circling overhead and gliding or sliding into a power dive.

Twenty five years ago they were on the verge of extinction in

Wales with a very poor breeding success rate. Their thin-shelled eggs would break under the sitting birds as a result of the accumulated effects of dieldrin compounds which built up in birds of prey every time they ate prey which had eaten the treated grain.

Thanks to the work carried out by Derek Ratcliffe and others the link between dieldrins and the poor breeding success of the peregrines was firmly established. There are probably about 25 pairs now breeding at suitable cliff sites throughout the mid Cambrian mountains and each year brings the discovery of new eyries.

I have seen a pair circling their nesting crag in misty March weather and a short time later watched the female brooding her eggs on a grassy ledge 10 or 15 metres up the cliff face. Another pair I was watching recently circled above a flock of pigeons funneling through the valley and dived repeatedly into the flock, completely confusing the disorientated pigeons, causing them to fly back and forth, unable to decide where to escape. The larger female caught a bird in its talons but failed to hold it. The pigeon dropped, then realised it was free and flew off, apparently unscathed. This unusual level of incompetence from one of these hooded executioners suggests that it was an immature bird which had not yet perfected its lethal arts. As often happens here in Wales, before seeing the peregrines the valley had been like an empty church, cold and silent but then immediately after seeing the peregrines we had displaying dipper fluttering and calling excitedly around us; a buzzard and kite circling the crests of the hills and four elegant grey wagtails, all seen from a small stonebridge within the space of three minutes or so.

Peregrines are quite noisy and betray their presence readily during the breeding season, so if you come across a pair, move off to a safe distance where you can watch them without disturbing them unduly.

One of the best known eyries is in **Cwmystwyth** above some derelict lead mines on a forbiddingly steep cliff face which would appear to be safe from any intruders but sadly it still gets robbed quite often, probably because it is too well known. The birds can regularly be seen from the mountain road below, as can be testified by the number of birdwatchers who stop and scan the cliffs with their binoculars.

Peregrines habitually take birds as large as, or even larger than themselves, their staple diet being birds like pigeons, gulls or curlew. I was surprised one year, however, to see one scoop up a young rabbit, rise steeply into the air and then drop the unfortunate animal, before diving down after it again.

Anywhere you come across steep, likely looking cliffs, you stand a fair chance of finding a peregrine. Listen for its chattering alarm note which is uttered with bold regularity.

A while ago, climbing a steep slope in the hills I came upon a cliff ledge with a rowan tree clinging tenaciously to the rocks and a female kestrel flew out of it off four reddish-mottled eggs. This nest was only a few hundred yards from a peregrine's eyrie with young. Strangely enough, in much of Ceredigion the kestrel (as mentioned on page 19) nests only on cliff ledges and never in trees.

Like the peregrine, raven or wheatear, the ring ouzel or mountain blackbird is also an inhabitant of rocky slopes but

Ring
Ouzel

left
Young
Teal

unfortunately this species appears to be getting scarcer and is not all that easy to find.

On a wet May day I found myself on a deep Breconshire pass looking for ring ouzel following a 'tip off' from an elderly bird watcher I had met not long before.

I clambered up a steep slope almost to the top and then worked my way down a steep gully. Then, way above me I heard the loud chinking notes of a male bird who flipped from one rock to another. The white crescent on his throat and flecks on his blackish plumage distinguished him clearly from a blackbird and his voice — sometimes a loud song, then the chinking notes, were quite different.

I returned to the area a fortnight later and found a comfortable place to sit about half way up the slope and kept my eyes open for the birds for I now hoped to see the pair. This time I was with a companion and our watching was soon rewarded when we were able to observe the ring ouzel pair flying to and from their nesting rock, taking food to their young. The site was on an outcrop about 2 metres high and partially covered with heather. There was an old nest close by and I wouldn't be surprised if this was a regular haunt of the mountain blackbird year after year.

Higher on the moors birds are scarcer but there are pockets of bird life and some interesting species can be found.

The red grouse is nowhere as common as it is, say, on the northern Pennines, partly because sheep have cropped the vegetation, denuding it of the heather and other plants on which this bird thrives. Nevertheless there are places you can still find them; on the heather moors north of Cwmystwyth, or near peat pools to the south which still have large heather patches, on **Plynlimon**, above the Elan Valley, near **Rhandirmwyn** by the upper Tywi. On the Radnor heather moors it is not scarce but in Montgomery it has declined seriously over the past decades with small numbers at places like Plymlimon, **Glaslyn** and **Bugeilyn**.

Snipe and curlew are more common on the rougher or boggier marginal land at lower altitudes but they may also be found on such ground at higher levels.

A car drive above the Elan Valley and along the mountain road to Aberystwyth will give opportunities to see a number of waders. Apart from snipe and curlew there are some lapwing and a few redshank which are often to be seen close to the river Elan. The calls of the common sandpiper as it bobs characteristically up and down are also usually to be heard by this and other mountain streams. Both the sandpiper and the snipe inhabit the high peat pools and tarns and are the most likely waders to be seen. The highlight of a day's birdwatching on the lonely moors, however, is the discovery of the golden plover or the dunlin in their highland habitat.

Both species are scarce, and random searching over endless moors is likely to prove both exhausting and frustrating. In Ceredigion both species may be looked for near peat bogs north-east or south-east of the Teifi lakes, or in Breconshire in the neighbourhood of **Drygarn Fawr**, the highest point in the north of that district. There are other haunts too in that general vicinity, near the **Claerwen** and Elan Valley Dams.

Golden plover seek out high places and are perhaps most easily seen on the ridges near Plynlimon in Ceredigion and Montgomery. Llanbrynmair may also have golden plover but the wholesale planting of conifers has done nothing to help either the plover or the red grouse which used to be found in good numbers here.

On Plynlimon last April, I was walking near the summit when I was fortunate enough to see a trip of 11 dotterel land in front of me. They ran about among the stones and scant vegetation sometimes tamely approaching to within 20 metres of where I was sitting, almost oblivious of my presence. Several of them were almost in full summer plumage and I wondered whether any might breed this year on the hills of Snowdonia as they have been proved to do in the last twenty years. Even nearer to home, the thought occurred that breeding could easily occur on mountain plateaux such as those of the Cader Idris no more than 20 miles from where I was watching them.

In search of Dunlin and Golden Plover

There is a mountain road leading through barren rocky country onto the hills above the Teifi lakes.

Leaving our car in a natural layby we set out to the north east, climbing steadily, following the sheep paths, skirting the soggy reed patches where possible, heading for the distant peaks which at 600 metres or so, are only a hundred metres higher than our present position. The distance shortens agonisingly slowly for we are keen to reach the lakes and peat pools which are our destination. The occasional raven or buzzard attracts our attention, and sometimes we look back at the Teifi lakes, now receding slowly into the distance.

At last we reach our objective, coming quickly upon it from the side of a slope, topped with a thin covering of bilberry plants. Below us now in the clear morning light we see the lake and in front of it a large area of brackish peat ditches sometimes opening out into pools with heather tufted islets. We scan the blackish mud eagerly but see no sign of a dunlin. A pair of sandpiper call noisily from a far shore, a red grouse croaks out its guttural rattle and then whirs in front of us across the bog before disappearing behind a heather clump. On the distant lake, there is a stir on the water as a male teal chases his

Dunlin

mate a few yards near the edge of the water.

A fresh breeze is getting up and making it harder to hold our binoculars steady or listen for birds. I then just made out the descending reel of a bird some way off. No, I had not imagined it, there it was again. I beckoned to my friend and we made our way quickly towards the sound.

There, standing still, close to a small pool, we saw what we had been looking for. A small black-bellied wader, with a slightly curved beak. This was our first summer Dunlin for the area, and our walk had been well rewarded.

Dunlin sometimes stand quietly by the water's edge for long periods with not a sign of movement. Amongst so much peat and boggy terrain such a small wader is easily overlooked. It often remains still even though the passer by may walk quite close to it. So we were extremely fortunate to locate this solitary bird.

A few days later and we were on the moors again, but the mist was low on the hills as we ascended them. The sunny weather below had lulled us into a false sense of security and we looked back anxiously, plotting our position using the familiar shape of the Teifi lakes and any hill, rock or other landmark which might assist our return.

Soon we were in the mists however, and now had to put our faith in our compass and our sense of direction.

It was only a matter of time before icy rain, seeping down our necks and soaking our clothing, made the going even more uncomfortable. We were off course and should have long since reached our destination. Thankfully with our compasses we surely couldn't be too far out; we moved our direction to the left, and suddenly put up a golden plover, startled from the slope of a hill. We would have been more excited had we known where we were!

If you are out on the hills and there is any doubt whatsoever about the weather conditions do be sure to be well equipped. You will need stout boots, rainwear, a compass and, unlike us on this occasion, an ordnance survey map! Don't forget, weather can change quickly on this high land.

Walking on, we were becoming increasingly apprehensive. Then, almost imperceptibly at first, the sound of squabbling black headed gulls became more audible. Could this be the colony at Llyn Ddu? Suddenly we were at the lake and a reconnoitre up and down the shore revealed the second small colony at the far side, which we knew existed. Breathing a sigh of relief, for we were beginning to feel miserable, we walked on.

A single, almost mournful, piping call caught our attention. The rain had stopped, visibility was improving slightly and we were more optimistic. Approaching the brow of the hill above a peat bog where there was a thin covering of bilberry and a few wisps of heather, there it was standing out conspicuously on a mossy hummock — a golden plover in its home territory. The weather was much brighter now, and the sunlight reflected on his golden flecked back. Soon we delighted in watching him and his mate who had appeared from nowhere. The golden plover has a charm of its own, and ranks high among my list of favourite birds.

For a while we watched the pair anxiously running to and fro and calling to each other. We retreated some way off, but could see no sign of the young through our binoculars. Not wishing to disturb them further, for they, like us, had had enough to contend with from inclement weather that day, we made off. The landmarks guiding us home were at last more visible. There was now a hazy light in front of us, and a sweet tang to the mountain air. Our spirits were lifted by the scenery, the view of those ageless hills on both sides now looking an uncanny bluish colour, receding in layers into the distance. We would walk these hills again in search of moorland waders another day.

In search of the Merlin

It is very fitting that a book entitled 'In Search of Birds' should finish with perhaps the most elusive of them all, the merlin. Unfortunately this species has become very scarce and there are probably no more than 60 pairs left in the whole of Wales. There are a few pairs in Ceredigion and the same is true for all the other county districts of mid Wales, perhaps 25 or 30 pairs in all, while the total Welsh population is about double this figure.

Merlin nest either in heather, grass, or other vegetation on the moor or in a moorland tree. They prefer areas close to the river valleys and the threat to their habitat of afforestation of these valleys is one which must be watched carefully. The merlin is just about the only British raptor which is currently on the decline.

We had seen merlin on three occasions last spring. One flew over us down the valley closing its wings and dropping momentarily in a bounding manner, characteristic of merlins. This was a female, but we had also followed a male as it flew along a country road in front of us for a third of a mile before veering off along a country track.

We were hoping to see a pair on their territory and the third one had looked more promising. He had flown from a low stone wall at the side of the road in a narrow river valley. Half an hour later when we returned to the spot he flew up again, this time climbing steeply into the blue sky like a jet plane. He circled at high speed and then hurtled earthwards, at the last moment braking to land in the bracken on the opposite side of the valley again. In autumn we have seen merlins on posts and trees in the hills and in winter when there is too little bird life in the uplands to feed them, I have even come across one watching for prey as it sat on the beach shingle. In summer a bird can be seen dashing across the moor, then in a flash it is gone, and could turn up almost anywhere miles away.

This merlin in the narrow valley had, as we said, looked promising and we hoped to track him down to his home territory. It was April when we had seen him the first time but this year we drew a blank. May wasn't much better either until, towards Whitsun, we spotted the female. She appeared in the distance at first looking almost no bigger than a skylark. As she approached closer, the shorter tail and darker brown plumage distinguished her from a golden plover kestrel. She hovered, wings beating strongly, then glided and flew

51

past us as we sat on the river bank, all too soon out of sight.

A few days later I stood in a copse a mile away watching redpolls and siskins high in the trees above me. I was hoping for a glimpse at least of the merlin and this I had when he rushed between the trees, flew high over a nearby hill and circled once before gliding beyond my view onto the moors.

We returned again to the spot in early July but there were no signs of the merlin. Exhaustive foot slogging across the local moors achieved nothing except aching feet and worn boot leather. Then, picking our way carefully down a gulley, for the slope was steep and slippery, we suddenly saw the male merlin chattering in alarm above a spruce plantation. I dismissed this as a potential nesting site for the merlin. Instead my eye caught the silhouette of the female merlin who had now joined her mate over the nearby moor and, after a minute's aerial display, they both zoomed down into the deep grass and bracken.

We watched the pair fly over the moor and round the wood on two more circuits, but the hour was by now late and we reluctantly returned to base.

The next day saw us at the same spot again. Merlin watching was becoming an addiction and we couldn't miss out on this wonderful chance to study the pair closely. Despite our serious reservations about the wood itself, we kept a good distance from the places the merlins were seen agitating, just in case the nest was close by.

We settled down, partially hidden in tall grass now dried out in the sunshine of the past few days. This was fairly near the gulley from where we had first seen the merlins the day before. The sound of the trickling stream was invigorating and yet relaxing, a sound I have always loved, as the water threaded its way between boulders and banks surmounted with rowan or mountain ash, now laden with red berries. A whinchat with his orange/pink breast and white eyestripe attracted our attention and a meadow pipit fluttered past. A pair of magpies chattered hoarsely as they flew across the valley. Then, out of the blue the male bird appeared and we were surprised to see him concentrating his attention once again on the fir plantation. Once he flew close to the deep grass where we were sitting and landed on a small rock, showing his blue grey back and reddish underparts. He flew back to the plantation 500 metres away rapping out his alarm note.

At times over the next 2 or 3 hours the female appeared and sometimes they flew round the wood together or chased each other over the moors.

We had been in this idyllic place for hours and it was nearing the time for us to move. As we walked along the small road at the side of the plantation late in the afternoon raucous noises met our ears from the spruce trees. A young jay or magpie perhaps? As we got nearer to the sound, only then did it occur to us: this was no jay or magpie. This must be a young merlin, although the trees were thick and only 5 metres or so high. So this was why the merlins had shown so much interest in the firs. We approached quietly through the trees. There above us was a nest near the top of a spruce with excreta splattered thickly from top to bottom of the sapling and on the ground, too, beneath the tree. There, on a high branch at the side of the nest which we could see had a strange woven basket-like rim encircling it, stood a rather ruffled looking juvenile merlin!

In other places merlins usually lay their eggs in scrapes among heather and other moorland vegetation but in mid Wales the nests of crows and other birds are frequently occupied. The use of a spruce tree in a thick plantation only 10 metres from the road, we must admit, did surprise us. Such a choice could augur well for the merlin if it proved readily acceptable, but its recent decline belies such optimism. At any rate this pair was successful in fledging its young,

Merlin

or at least one of them, in unlikely surroundings. Time will show whether the merlins will return again.

THE MOORLANDS are the last of our seven habitats. We have treated each of them separately but of course most places in which you might find yourself will have a mixture of them close at hand. You may be walking by a river, with a wooded hillside on one bank, farmland on the far side and a spruce plantation beyond that; or on the edge of a moor, with a plantation adjacent to it and an upland lake nearby. Obviously where there is a combination of habitats you will see a greater variety of birds.

Bird watchers in mid Wales are still thin on the ground and new data is always welcome to add to our knowledge. There is always a chance that you will find something new and exciting. We wish you good luck in your search for birds in mid Wales and equally, much pleasure from the wonderful countryside surrounding you.

grey wagtail

Check List of Breeding Birds, Status and Distribution according to Habitat

The list below covers those birds which breed regularly or have done so occasionally in mid Wales over the past 40 years.

There are very real problems in assessing the abundance or rarity of each species. We have provided a 1–5 point scale and marked each regular nesting species on this, a rating of 1 being the most abundant and 5 the scarcest. Our assessment is based primarily on personal observation and partly on information gathered from reports.

Our ratings are certainly not based directly on any survey and we would not claim them to be the last word on the subject. It is also difficult to make comparisons, since a bird like a shelduck which is conspicuous, large and confined to a restricted habitat, subjectively is not looked upon as rare, though there are perhaps only twenty pairs. The same numbers of crossbills, for example, in the pine forests would scarcely be noticed.

So our list should be seen only as a guide. On a full day's birdwatching in suitable habitats and at the right time of the year, you would expect to see (or hear) all of those species in category 1 and most of those in category 2 or 2+. Some of those in 3 would be quite hard to find or you would need rather more luck, except for those which have a restricted habitat. Species in category 4 you will normally find less often and you may have to make a special effort to find them. Remember the ratings are of breeding birds and some, like the starling, teal or dunlin, are very much commoner as winter visitors, or on migration.

There are some rare British birds in category 5 but several of them, as it happens, are common enough over the border. Such birds include great crested grebe, reed warbler, turtle dove, common

Goshawk

partridge, and, of course, the very familiar mute swan. No category has been assigned to those species which are sporadic or have ceased to breed in mid Wales and these are marked with an asterisk.

Unless described as a summer visitor, it should be assumed a species is an all year round resident in the British Isles. Many of these do, of course, leave their summer habitats to seek food or shelter elsewhere. Some form feeding flocks like the finches, others, like many of the waders, feed on the coasts and estuaries. Very few birds are still to be found on the mountains in wintertime.

Finally we have recorded, using a 1–7 code, the habitats in which each species is to be found breeding, and is therefore most likely to be encountered. Some species, notably the birds of prey, feed in habitats away from their nests. The kite, for example, habitually hunts over moorland, upland lakes and high sheep walks, the goshawk is as likely to be seen over the mountainous country as in the forests.

Status		Habitat	
Category 1	– *Abundant*	**1**	– *The coast*
Category 2	– *Common*	**2**	– *Marsh and estuary*
Category 2+	– *Fairly Common*		*(including low*
Category 3	– *Uncommon*		*lakes)*
Category 4	– *Scarce*	**3**	– *Farmland*
Category 5	– *Very Scarce*	**4**	– *Rivers and Upland Lakes*
		5	– *Valley and Upland Woods*
		6	– *Conifer Plantations*
		7	– *Uplands, moors and mountains.*

			STATUS	HABITAT
1	**Great Crested Grebe**	Two or three pairs usually nest in Ceredigion, and rather more in Montgomery and Radnor.	5	2.4
2	**Little Grebe**	Breeds in small numbers, mostly on lower lakes and pools. Nowhere is this species common.	4	2.4
3	**Fulmar**	Expanding numbers since it first brd in 1947 and now there are well over 200 pairs breeding on suitable cliffs.	2+	1

4	**Cormorant**	Several breeding colonies along the coast, the largest at Penderi (usually about 150 pairs). Inland colony at Craig yr Aderyn in south Merioneth.	2	1
5	**Shag**	Resident but much scarcer than the last species breeding thinly on suitable cliffs from Penderi southwards.	3	1
6	**Grey Heron**	There are scattered colonies, rarely of more than 12 or 15 pairs mostly associated with river systems throughout mid Wales.	2+	2.3.4.5
7	**Mute Swan**	Scarce resident, found on the Teifi, the Severn, the Wye and one or two other sites in eastern areas.	5	2
8	**Canada Goose**	Breeds widely eastern Montgomery, and a few pairs in Radnor and Ceredigion.	5	2
9	**Shelduck**	Small numbers breed on the estuaries of the Dyfi, Mawddach, Dysynni, Teifi and occasionally elsewhere.	3	1
10	**Mallard**	Common, on marshes and rivers everywhere.	2	2.4
11	**Teal**	Nests regularly but thinly near lakes and pools in many upland areas. Probably commoner in Ceredigion than elsewhere.	4	2.4
12	**Tufted Duck**	Resident. Breeds regularly in very small numbers in Radnor and Montgomery but not elsewhere.	5	2 .
13	**Shoveler**	Bred Tregaron Bog on two or three occasions in the last 30 years and once at Ynishir.	–	–

cormorant

14	**Garganey**	One breeding record only — Tregaron in 1968	–	–
15	**Red Breasted Merganser**	Resident, mostly Dyfi area and further north in Merioneth.	4	**1.4**
16	**Goosander**	Now establishing itself firmly after it first bred in Montgomery in 1970. Breeds on some of the larger lakes and several rivers, including Severn, Tywi, Wye, Rheidol, Ystwyth and Cothi.		**4.5.1**
17	**Peregrine Falcon**	There are perhaps 40 or 50 pairs breeding in the area covered by the map, divided between coastal sites and inland crags.	4	**1.7**
18	**Hobby**	Bred in Radnor 1962 & 1963, and may have done so occasionally there and elsewhere on other occasions. Not uncommonly seen in summer.	*	
19	**Kestrel**	Breeds on coast and inland cliffs in Ceredigion, but in woodlands, too, in eastern parts of mid Wales.	3	**1.3.7**
20	**Merlin**	Small numbers breed widely on the moors (maybe 25 pairs). Has decreased in recent years; formerly nested on coastal slopes.	4	**7**
21	**Buzzard**	The most numerous bird of prey, found throughout the area but most commonly in or near the Cambrian Hills.	2	**1.3.5.6.7**
22	**Red Kite**	About 40 pairs in wooded districts, this being virtually the total British population of the species.	4	**5**

Sedge w[...]

58

23	Sparrow Hawk	Widely distributed and quite common in woods, both conifer and deciduous.	3	3.5.6
24	Goshawk	Pairs have been proved breeding in the forests of north Carmarthenshire and Breconshire and birds are seen regularly elsewhere.	5	5.6
25	Hen Harrier	A few pairs breed regularly in north Montgomery. The only recent nesting record for Ceredigion was in 1972 (but see text)	5	6.7
26	Montagus Harrier	Has bred occasionally in the past but now less likely since the species has declined in its strongholds elsewhere in Britain.	*	
27	Red Grouse	Numbers limited by sparseness of heather on the moors. Commoner in Radnor and Brecon, has decreased in Montgomery. Smaller numbers in Ceredigion and north Carmarthen	4	7
28	Black Grouse	Breeds thinly and locally, mostly where there is heather and bilberry in young conifer plantations.	4	6.7
29	Common Partridge	Scarce and decreasing, mostly in lower lying areas and commoner in the east.	5	3
30	Red Legged Partridge	Scarce, occurring only in eastern-most areas where rarely encountered.	5	3
31	Quail	Breeds very occasionally, certainly not annually and could turn up anywhere in agricultural country with crops or mowing grass.	5	3

32	**Pheasant**	Resident, fairly common though local.	2	3.5
33	**Water rail**	Probably regular breeder though scarce and rarely proved to do so.	5	2
34	**Spotted Crake**	Scarce visitor mostly in spring, suspected of having bred Cors Caron (Tregaron Bog) and Dyfi in the past	*	2
		and has certainly done so in Radnor at Rhosgoch.		
35	**Corncrake**	Formerly common on farmland, now very scarce summer visitor and nearly extinct as a breeding species.	*	3
36	**Moorhen**	Surprisingly uncommon throughout the area. Avoids higher ground.	3	2.3
37	**Coot**	Thinly but widely distributed, the odd pair or two on most of the hill lakes and lower pools.	2	2.4
38	**Oyster Catcher**	Breeds fairly commonly along the coast.	2+	1
39	**Lapwing**	Fairly thin on the ground as a resident species, numbers have declined.	2+	2.3.4.7
40	**Golden Plover**	Small numbers breed on the highest moors, commoner on the eastern side of the Cambrians.	4	7
41	**Ringed Plover**	Breeds on dunes and shingle banks between the Mawddach estuary and Borth.	4	1
42	**Dunlin**	A small number of pairs frequent upland bogs and pools in spring and summer.	4	7

43	**Snipe**	Breeds on marshes and wet sites in many places.	2+	**2.3.4.7**
44	**Woodcock**	Not scarce, mostly east of the Cambrians but also at Ynyshir reserve north of the Dyfi estuary and sometimes elsewhere.	3	5
45	**Curlew**	Fairly common, the curlew is the most plentiful of the waders.	2+	**2.3.4.7**
46	**Redshank**	Breeds by the Dyfi and in south Merioneth, also elsewhere on a few upland marshes and lower lying wetlands.	4	**2.7**
47	**Common Sandpiper**	Common summer visitor by streams and upland lakes.	3	**4.7**
48	**Great Black Back**	Some pairs breed here and there along the coast.	3	1
49	**Lesser Black Back**	The odd pair or two breed on the coast, mostly in the south. There is a colony of this species on Cardigan Island.	4	1
50	**Herring Gull**	Common on coastal cliffs where it is found in colonies.	1	1
51	**Kittiwake**	Breeds in two or three places in the south. Loch Tyn colony holds about 80 pairs.	3	1
52	**Black Headed Gull**	There are colonies nesting on many pools and lakes in the hills and one or two places elsewhere at lower level.	2	**2.4**
	Little Tern	A few pairs until recently, found in south Merioneth.		

common snipe

61

53	**Guillimot**	Breeds in several places from New Quay Head south.	3	1
54	**Razorbill**	Found from New Quay Head southwards but in smaller numbers than guillimot.	3	1
55	**Rock Dove**	Mixed with feral stock but found on various coastal cliffs.	3	1
56	**Stock Dove**	Widespread resident.	3	3
57	**Wood Pigeon**	Numerous, especially in conifer woods.	1	3.5.6
58	**Collared Dove**	Common in towns and villages — started breeding about 1960.	2	3
59	**Turtle Dove**	Very scarce summer visitor. A few pairs breed in eastern Powys.	*	
60	**Cuckoo**	Widespread summer visitor though not especially common	2+	3.5.6.7
61	**Barn Owl**	Widespread but quite scarce	3	3
62	**Little Owl**	Scarce species, commoner in eastern Powys than elsewhere.	5	3
63	**Tawny Owl**	Common resident.	2	3.5
64	**Long Eared Owl**	Rare resident. This elusive bird most likely in north Brecon, Radnor Forest and north Montgomery. Has bred in Ceredigion.	5	3.5.6
65	**Short Eared owl**	Sometimes nests in the uplands, particularly on young fir plantations. Most frequent north	5	6.7

Kingfisher

		Montgomery and north Brecon especially Mynydd Eppynt		
66	**Nightjar**	Very scarce summer visitor. The only regular site now is the reserve at Ynyshir where two or three pairs nested until recently. Apparently decreasing, but could be overlooked.	5	5.6
67	**Swift**	Common Summer visitor.	2	3
68	**Kingfisher**	Scarce in the West, commoner on the gentler streams and lower ground to the East of the Cambrians such as the Severn Valley.	4	4
69	**Green Wood-pecker**	Uncommon resident	3	3.5
70	**Great Spotted Wood-pecker**	Fairly common in woodlands.	2+	3.5.6
71	**Lesser Spotted Wood-pecker**	Quite scarce, most frequent in lower wooded valleys.	4	3.5
72	**Woodlark**	Former uncommon resident, appears to have been absent as a nesting bird for the last 15-20 years.	*	
73	**Skylark**	Common, especially in upland districts	2	2.3.7
74	**Sand-martin**	Widely scattered summer visitor, usually in small colonies in banks of rivers.	2+	4
75	**House Martin**	Common Summer visitor	2	3

76	Swallow	Very common Summer visitor.	1	3
77	Raven	Common on coastal cliffs, inland crags, and in woodlands.	2+	1.5.6.7
78	Carrion Crow	Abundant in all districts.	1	1.3.5
79	Rook	Plentiful especially in coastal areas and lower sheltered valleys.	1	3.5
80	Jackdaw	Breeds commonly in cliff crevices or tunnels, in old ruins, barns and holes in trees.	1	1.3.5
81	Chough	Scarce, found mostly on coastal cliffs but a few pairs breed inland in Ceredigion, south Merioneth and west Montgomery.	4	1.7
82	Magpie	Very abundant species on agricultural land.	1	1.3
83	Jay	Common woodland bird especially in conifer woods.	2	3.5.6
84	Great Tit	Abundant, perhaps even more so than blue tit in some places.	1	3.5
85	Blue Tit	Abundant resident	1	3.5.6
86	Coal Tit	Common, particularly in conifer woods	1	5.6
87	Marsh Tit	Fairly common, usually avoids higher ground. Quite scarce in north Ceredigion.	2	3.4.5
88	Willow Tit	Quite common, rather scarcer than marsh tit, except in North Ceredigion.	2+	3.5.4
89	Long Tailed Tit	Widespread and common.	2	3.5.6

90	**Nuthatch**	Frequent in deciduous woodland where it is often one of the characteristic species.	2+	3.6
91	**Tree Creeper**	Fairly widespread and common.	2	3.5
92	**Wren**	Numerous resident breeder except after hard winters when numbers are greatly reduced.	1	1.5.6
93	**Dipper**	Typical and fairly common bird of streams and rivers. May have decreased lately.	3	4
94	**Mistle Thrush**	Common and widespread resident.	2	3.5
95	**Song Thrush**	Commoner in lower more sheltered areas than the above species but scarcer at higher levels.	1	3.5.6
96	**Blackbird**	Abundant.	1	3.5
97	**Ring Ouzel**	Scarce breeding bird, in high rocky places.	4	7
98	**Wheatear**	Summer visitor. Most numerous in upland rocky valleys and slopes, some pairs also found at the coast.	2	1.7
99	**Stonechat**	Resident. Commoner on coast than inland. A few pairs also breed on commons and hillsides with gorse and heather elsewhere in mid Wales.	3	1.7
100	**Whinchat**	Summer visitor. Not scarce in rough pasture, marginal upland places, marsh and upland valleys with bracken and bushes, etc.	2+	2.3.6.7
101	**Robin**	Abundant resident.	1	3.5.6

102	Redstart	Fairly common summer visitor in upland woods, valleys and open ground with a scatter of trees.	2+	3.4.5
103	Grass-hopper Warbler	Uncommon summer visitor, mostly in marsh and wetlands and on plantations.	3	2.6
104	Reed-warbler	During the past few years has started to breed in the Dyfi area—a few pairs only. Like virtually all the warblers here, a Summer visitor. All breeds near Teifi and Mawddach estuaries.	5	2
105	Sedge Warbler	Local summer visitor.	3	2
106	Lesser White-throat	Scarce summer visitor. Just a few pairs in coastal districts but more in Radnor and Montgomery.	4	3
107	White-throat.	Summer visitor. Common on agricultural land on lower ground.	2	3
108	Garden Warbler	Widespread Summer visitor, fairly common even in suitable highland woods.	2	3.5
109	Blackcap	Summer visitor (occasionally winters). Scarcer than the last species, the blackcap is more restricted to sheltered places.	2+	3.5
110	Willow Warbler	Abundant summer visitor.	1	3.5.6
111	Chiffchaff	Summer visitor. Fairly common in lower lying woodlands with adequate undergrowth.	2	3.5.6
112	Wood Warbler	Summer visitor. Common and typical species of	2	3.5

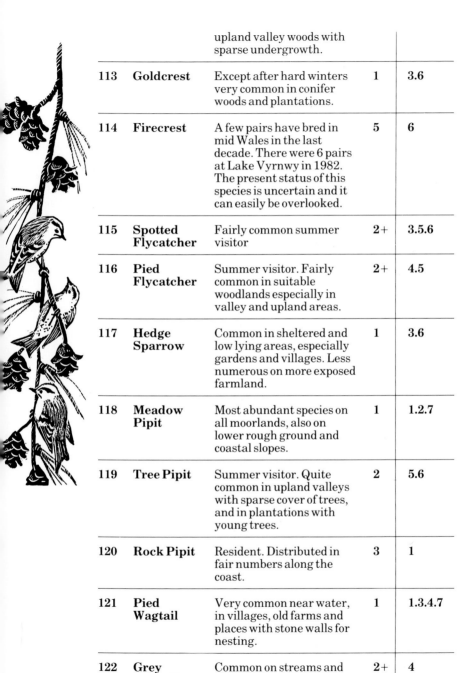

		upland valley woods with sparse undergrowth.		
113	**Goldcrest**	Except after hard winters very common in conifer woods and plantations.	1	**3.6**
114	**Firecrest**	A few pairs have bred in mid Wales in the last decade. There were 6 pairs at Lake Vyrnwy in 1982. The present status of this species is uncertain and it can easily be overlooked.	5	**6**
115	**Spotted Flycatcher**	Fairly common summer visitor	2+	**3.5.6**
116	**Pied Flycatcher**	Summer visitor. Fairly common in suitable woodlands especially in valley and upland areas.	2+	**4.5**
117	**Hedge Sparrow**	Common in sheltered and low lying areas, especially gardens and villages. Less numerous on more exposed farmland.	1	**3.6**
118	**Meadow Pipit**	Most abundant species on all moorlands, also on lower rough ground and coastal slopes.	1	**1.2.7**
119	**Tree Pipit**	Summer visitor. Quite common in upland valleys with sparse cover of trees, and in plantations with young trees.	2	**5.6**
120	**Rock Pipit**	Resident. Distributed in fair numbers along the coast.	3	**1**
121	**Pied Wagtail**	Very common near water, in villages, old farms and places with stone walls for nesting.	1	**1.3.4.7**
122	**Grey Wagtail**	Common on streams and rivers.	2+	**4**

goldcrests

123	Yellow Wagtail	Summer visitor. Breeds sporadically in river valleys such as the Teme and Severn in the east.	5	2
124	Starling	Fairly common as a breeding species in towns, but quite scarce in the country, especially in the west.	2+	3.5
125	House Sparrow	Common in towns and villages but by no means numerous.	1	3
126	Tree Sparrow	Breeds in small numbers locally east of main Cambrian chain, but rarely in the west and then usually north of Aberystwyth.	4	3
127	Greenfinch	Fairly common in sheltered or low lying districts with shrubberies and gardens.	2+	3
128	Goldfinch	Quite common especially in lanes, hedgerows with farmsteads etc. especially where there is rough ground nearby.	2+	3.2
129	Linnet	Fairly common, notably near the coast, also on fairly high ground where there is gorse and scrub.	2	1.3.7
130	Siskin	A new breeding species just establishing itself in spruce and other conifer plantations on the hills and in valleys. Commoner in Winter.	3	6
131	Redpoll	Fairly common, mostly frequenting fir plantations or small stands of birch, willow, alder, etc. in areas bordering the hills.	2+	5.6
132	Hawfinch	A few pairs probably breed in Montgomery and	5	3.5

		Radnor. Hawfinches are easily overlooked.		
133	**Bullfinch**	Not uncommon in areas with scrub, bramble and suchlike vegetation including plantations, railway cuttings etc.	3	**3.6**
134	**Chaffinch**	Probably the most abundant species in mid Wales in all kinds of woodland and farmland habitat.	1	**3.5.6**
135	**Crossbill**	Breeds sparingly in conifer plantations in Montgomery, South Merioneth, North Brecon, Radnor Forest and elsewhere. Has bred a few times in Ceredigion and inevitably overlooked.	5	**6**
137	**Yellow Hammer**	Fairly common, especially in gorse and on bracken hillsides, plantations and places with rough low-growing vegetation.	2	**3.6**
138	**Reed Bunting**	Local but widely distributed species on marshy ground.	3	**2**

Bird names in Welsh

1. Gwyach Fawr Gopog
2. Gwyach Fach
3. Aderyn-Drycin y Graig
4. Mulfran
5. Mulfran Werdd
6. Crëyr Glas
7. Alarch Dof
8. Gŵydd Canada
9. Hwyaden yr Eithin
10. Hwyaden Wyllt
11. Corhwyaden
12. Hwyaden Gopog
13. Hwyaden Lydanbig
14. Hwyaden Addfain
15. Hwyaden Frongoch
16. Hwyaden Dramor
17. Hebog Glas
18. Hebog yr Ehedydd
19. Cudyll Coch
20. Cudyll Bach
21. Bwncath
22. Barcud
23. Gwalch Glas
24. Gwyddwalch
25. Boda Tinwen
26. Boda Montagu
27. Grugiar
28. Grugiar Ddu
29. Petrisen
30. Petrisen Goesgoch
31. Sofliar
32. Ffesant
33. Rhegen y Dŵr
34. Rhegen Fraith
35. Rhegen yr Yd
36. Iâr Ddŵr
37. Cwtiar
38. Pioden y Môr
39. Cornchwiglen
40. Cwtiad Aur
41. Cwtiad Torchog
42. Pibydd y Mawn
43. Giach Gyffredin
44. Cyffylog
45. Gylfinir
46. Pibydd Coesgoch
47. Pibydd y Dorlan
48. Gwylan Gefnddu Fwyaf
49. Gwylan Gefnddu Leiaf
50. Gwylan y Penwaig
51. Gwylan Goesddu
52. Gwylan Benddu
53. Gwylog
54. Llurs
55. Colomen y Craig
56. Colomen Wyllt
57. Ysguthan
58. Turtur Dorchog
59. Turtur
60. Cog
61. Tylluan Wen
62. Tylluan Fach
63. Tylluan Frech
64. Tylluan Gorniog
65. Tylluan Glustiog
66. Troellwr Mawr
67. Gwennol Ddu
68. Glas y Dorlan
69. Cnocell Werdd
70. Cnocell Fraith Fwyaf
71. Cnocell Fraith Leiaf
72. Ehedydd y Coed
73. Ehedydd
74. Gwennol y Glennydd
75. Gwennol y Bondo
76. Gwennol
77. Cigfran
78. Brân Dyddyn
79. Ydfran
80. Jac-y-do
81. Brân Goesgoch
82. Pioden
83. Ysgrech y Coed
84. Titw Mawr
85. Titw Tomos Las
86. Titw Penddu
87. Titw'r Wern
88. Titw'r Helyg
89. Titw Gynffon-hir
90. Delor y Cnau
91. Dringwr Bach
92. Dryw
93. Bronwen y Dŵr
94. Brych y Coed
95. Bronfraith
96. Mwyalchen
97. Mwyalchen y Mynydd
98. Tinwen y Garn
99. Clochdar y Cerrig
100. Crec yr Eithin
101. Robin Goch
102. Tingoch
103. Troellwr Bach
104. Telor y Cyrs
105. Telor yr Hesg
106. Llwyndron Fach
107. Llwyndron
108. Telor yr Ardd
109. Telor Penddu
110. Telor yr Helyg
111. Siff-saff
112. Telor y Coed
113. Dryw Eurben
114. Dryw Penfflamgoch
115. Gwybedog Mannog
116. Gwybedog Brith
117. Llwyd y Gwrych
118. Corhedydd y Waun
119. Corhedydd y Coed
120. Corhedydd y Craig
121. Siglen Fraith
122. Siglen Lwyd
123. Siglen Felen
124. Drudwen
125. Aderyn y To
126. Llwyd y Mynydd
127. Llinos Werdd
128. Nico
129. Llinos
130. Pila Gwyrdd
131. Llinos Frongoch
132. Gylfinbraff
133. Coch y Berllan
134. Ji-binc
135. Gylfin Groes
136. Morwennol Fechan
137. Bras Melyn
138. Bras y Cyrs

Useful addresses of organisations:

Nature Conservancy Council
*Dyfed-Powys Regional Officer, Plas Gogerddan,
Tel. Aberystwyth 828551*

Dyfed Wildlife Trust
7 Market Street, Haverfordwest.

RSPB (Wales Office)
Bryn Aderyn, The Bank, Newtown.

The Royal Society for the Protection of Birds
The Lodge, Sandy, Beds.